AMBITION

Ambition

How We
Manage Success
and Failure
Throughout Our Lives

Gilbert Brim

BasicBooks
A Division of HarperCollins*Publishers*

I wish to express my gratitude for permission to quote from:

The lines from "Greed" (translated by Stanley Kunitz) are reprinted from *Life Sentence, Selected Poems*, by Nina Cassian, edited by William Jay Smith, by permission of W. W. Norton & Company, Inc. Copyright © 1990 by Nina Cassian.

"The Armful" from *The Poetry of Robert Frost*, edited by Edward Connery Lathem. Copyright 1928, © 1969 by Holt, Rinehart and Winston. Copyright © 1956 by Robert Frost. Reprinted by permission of Henry Holt and Company, Inc.

"As I Walked Out One Evening" from *W. H. Auden: Collected Poems*, by W. H. Auden, edited by Edward Mendelson. Copyright 1940 and renewed 1968 by W. H. Auden. Reprinted by permission of Random House, Inc.

"Friday, August 1: Murphy's Sixth Corollary: Whenever you set out to do something, something else must be done first." Reprinted from *Murphy's Law Desk Calendar*, by Arthur Bloch. © 1977, 1982, 1984, 1985, with permission from Price Stern Sloan, Inc., Los Angeles.

Brim, Gilbert, 1923–
Ambition: how we manage success and failure throughout our lives/Gilbert Brim.
p. cm.
Includes bibliographical references and index.
ISBN 0-465-09190-3
1. Achievement motivation. 2. Success—psychological aspects. 3. Failure (Psychology) 4. Ambition. I. Title.
BF503.B75 1992   91-55453
155.2—dc20   CIP

Copyright © 1992 by Gilbert Brim
PRINTED IN THE UNITED STATES OF AMERICA
Designed by Ellen Levine
92 93 94 95 SWD/SS 9 8 7 6 5 4 3 2 1

Contents

Acknowledgments

Many friends helped in the creation of this book by giving steady encouragement and directions to important information, by reading various drafts along the way and responding with honest feedback and usable suggestions, and by occasionally providing an apt turn of phrase. I am especially grateful to: Paul B. Baltes, Paul Cleary, Howard E. Freeman, David A. Goslin, Judith Greissman, Patricia B. Gurin, Mary Agnes Hess, Margie E. Lachman, Wilbert J. McKeachie, Robert K. Merton, John Robert Newbrough, Alice S. Rossi, Carol D. Ryff, Richard Shweder, and Heidi Sigal.

Anne Rosenfeld drew on her wide experience as a professional editor to transform many awkward psychological paragraphs into statements that now are more interesting and pleasant to read. Martin Kessler at Basic Books found the time, in addition to his roles as president and editor-in-chief, to carry out an invaluable personal editing of the manuscript. Phoebe Hoss, the developmental editor, did the last line-by-line editing and correcting, along with some rewriting and rearranging to give the book its final polish.

At the beginning, Joan Pifer typed, formatted, and put in order the first, rough versions of the manuscript. Camille Yezzi typed a subsequent draft during one pivotal year. In the final writing, over a three-year period, Barbara Van Zandt, assisted by Brenda Theall, typed and corrected successive revisions with grace and dedication. My thanks to these close companions.

Thanks are due to the Social Science Research Council for my participation in a December 1983 conference in Santa Barbara on "Winning and Losing," where I first presented my ideas for this book, and I will always be indebted to the Russell Sage Foundation, which awarded me a year as a Visiting Scholar in 1985–86 so that I could begin my writing.

Prologue

My Father's Windowbox

My father was one hundred and three years old when he died several summers ago. He grew up on a farm in Ohio and was the only one of seven children to leave farming, finding his way through complicated paths to Harvard and to Columbia, getting his Ph.D. with John Dewey (in rural education), and teaching at Ohio State University until he was sixty. Then he and my mother bought an old abandoned farm of several hundred acres in northwest Connecticut, remodeled the house, and moved there to live.

He set about to clean the fence rows and to clear the woods the way he had been taught to do as a boy in Ohio. For many years he roamed the hillsides and mountaintop, thinning trees, trimming brush, and taking pride in looking up from the porch at his clean and tidy mountain. As he grew older, his legs and back would tire earlier in the day, and sometimes he would get a friend to help him or hire a young man to work with him to keep up the place.

Over the years, almost unnoticeably, the upper part of the mountain was no longer within his range; and gradually his level of aspiration lowered, coming down the hillside, so to speak, into the trees and land around the house with a new and large investment of energy in gardening, both vegetables and flowers.

At one time, when he had plots of asparagus and rows of raspberries and fields of gladioli, he would supply his friends throughout the northwest corner of Connecticut with armloads of "glads," as he called them. He cultivated his crops with a power tiller much like a lawnmower. Later, as it became harder for him to bear down on the handles to lift the tiller's front end to turn, the width between the rows grew larger. On his ninetieth birthday, he bought a small riding tractor.

One year he did not plant the gardens, and his attention turned to the little border flowers around the house and to four large outdoor windowboxes. At waist height, they required no knee bending to cultivate. The windowboxes served well for years, but then his failing sight and muscular strength meant that he could not tend even these without great effort. In the end, the tree work, farm work, and gardening all were given up. But he focused on a new activity: listening to "talking books"—novels, biographies of great poets, and a good sampling of the world's drama.

After a few minor strokes during his one hundred and second year, he could not see well enough to deal with television or hear well enough to use the talking books. His windowboxes were still there, and he would go outdoors to see them, dimly. He felt the soil and watered them when needed. Although planted by someone else, they still were his achievements. He would file his garden tools, especially his hoe, to keep them sharp; it was easy to do by touch.

Having seen the scope of his life shrink dramatically to its narrow compass ("There's so little left of me," he said), he told me he would like to leave—but not through his own action; he was waiting, and hoping.

This man was as happy and fulfilled at one hundred and one as he was at age sixty. In dealing with the gaps between his desires and achievements, he had an unyielding drive for growth and mastery, a rational mind, and a capacity for change. But these traits were not unique to my father; they are part of every human being.

This book is about human nature and ambition. It is about how we deal with our successes and failures in day-to-day life; about how we respond to winning and losing so that we keep growing and changing throughout our lives. It is about our ambition through life—about how we maintain it, how we increase it, how we control it, how we get rid of it. It is about what happens to us and our youthful dreams.

In part I, I present these fundamental truths about the range of ambition in human beings:

- We have a basic drive for growth and mastery that is expressed in a variety of specific ambitions. This is a universal character-istic of humans, shared equally by men and women, varying little in history or across different cultures. The goals we seek may be diverse—health, creativity, money, intimacy, helping others, doing good, and many more—but we are propelled by the same operating energy that is distinctive of humanity.
- We prefer to live in a way that keeps us at a level of "just man-ageable difficulties." We want to be challenged. If life is too hard, we try to ease back; but if life is too easy, we try to create greater challenges and put more demands upon ourselves.
- One of the important sources of human happiness is working on tasks at a suitable level of difficulty, neither too hard nor too easy. Almost regardless of position in life, it is possible to reorganize our lives after successes and failures so as to find new challenges. Therefore, there are no big differences in hap-piness between the rich and the poor, the healthy and the injured, the young and the old.

In part II, I begin with how we think about losing and winning: that is, how we find out about our successes and failures. Then I examine how we identify the causes of our wins and losses and plan what to do next. Our capacity to change during our lives is much greater than scientists used to believe was true. We make important changes through our lifespan, and the influences of events in our early years are continually transformed by our later experiences. Nevertheless, we must take into account the controls over our actions, both our personal standards and the opinions of others important to us.

The guiding idea in this section is that as humans we are for the most part purposeful and reasonable in our efforts to deal with our lives. Many of our thoughts are about intentions, purposes, mental maps, wishes, hopes, and beliefs. We create strategies of action to get what we want. Almost always what we are doing has a plan and a timetable.

A younger friend says that "most people can't tell what they are doing"; and that many of us do not have long-term life goals, but rather move from goal to goal, adapting as we achieve or do not achieve in a particular case. We look for doors to open, and slip through them, and then, in the next room, look for another door. But we can see only one room at a time. It is not clear until we get to one place that something else is now possible; before that, it was a secret, or we never saw it.

This description may apply to some of us some of the time, but most of us plan for the longer term. We have images of our life course, of where we expect to be and what we expect to be doing at times in our future. These visions of future life may be fuzzy. They may never come true. Nevertheless, we do have long-range goals and timetables for reaching them; and when taken all together they are a life plan, such as it is. As we succeed or fail, we revise time and time again. With experience and some abbreviations and perhaps a few diagrams, we can lay out this plan on a single page—a "life plan at a glance" in its hundredth revision.

In part III, I describe how we keep up the challenge: that is, the methods we use to manage winning or losing events in our lives. Winning or losing sets in motion a process of finding a new level of just manageable difficulty. There is no fixed point to which we return after each action; the level is always changing. The happiest among us keep the pressure turned up or down to that point where we have a challenge we believe we can manage. When we win, we try for more; when we fail, we cut back.

Our purposive actions have four elements:

- our desired goal;
- our aspirations—ideal, minimum, and realistic—for how much we will achieve;
- our timetable for how long it will take us to achieve our goal;
- our behavior, our means, for achieving the goal.

My father's transition from mountaintop to windowbox shows how, in dealing with losing, we try first to improve our behavior. Then we change our timetable, giving ourselves more time. We lower our level of aspiration. If we still fail, we leave this particular goal behind and move on to something more manageable. In dealing with winning, we use these methods, but in a different way. First, we rarely change behavior after winning. Instead, we shorten our timetables and speed up our plans for achievement. We raise our aspirations. We add new goals. In some ways, winning is harder to manage than losing.

When writing this book, I sometimes saw myself on a journey into a little-known region of human personality, equipped with crude maps and fragments of reports from earlier travelers, discovering unusual customs, people, experiences—"some strange and wondrous beasts."

I have drawn on the best of modern psychological and social science knowledge; on the world of sports, where the challenges of winning and losing are most clearly displayed; and on stories and cases from a variety of lives. Thus, on a walk through the upper east side of Manhattan, I have found the air thick with goals, aspirations, and dreams, with winning and losing: newsstand owners and taxi drivers, scanning the sidewalks for possible customers; joggers and marathoners running back and forth to the park; old ladies teetering across the street, trying to reach the corner before the light changes; homeless men and women with their heads in trash baskets groping for something of value; a two-year-old looking ahead for his grandfather's appearance around the street corner, and his mother wishing for the child's good behavior when they do meet.

If what I say here seems at times familiar, it is purposeful. I believe that the familiar, what we think we already know, can often have an unexpected twist. Analyzing ambition in everyday life is like refracting it through a prism, yielding new and unexpected insights. I offer them here not in an attempt to tell others how to live, but in the belief that—however different our images of human nature—we can direct our own lives better for knowing about how human beings manage success and failure.

I

The Range
of Ambition

1

Our Drive for Growth and Mastery

Psychologists studying chimpanzees have shown that chimps and other primates will work hard at problems for no other reward than being permitted to see, hear, or handle something in their environment.* Young primates are motivated to explore the world around them, to expand their territory, to control their life as best they can, and to flee from what they cannot control. Over a long time, evolution and natural selection will favor those chimps with these behavior patterns because they can manage new and strange life events.

At a lower level of evolution, rats show the same curiosity and exploration. Many years ago in the football stadium at the University of California, Berkeley, during the winter, a graduate student in psychology sat on a bench halfway up the deserted stadium and opened the door of a carrying cage in which he had brought a white rat. Thirty minutes passed. The rat left the cage for a few seconds, then re-entered, and stayed in the cage. The

*This and all other references are to be found in the unnumbered notes beginning on page 177. Any unattributed quotations are those I have gathered personally.

9

next day, the curious rat left the cage for a longer period and explored several feet away. A week afterward, the rat had covered the distance down to the field and back; and a month later, as soon as the cage door was opened, the rat ran down the steps, across the football field, up the steps on the other side of the stadium, and then halfway around the stadium to return to its cage. All of this occurred without any of the obvious rewards of food pellets, water, or stroking.

So it is for humans, too, who have ventured out from their ancient African origin to cover the earth. The image of primitive beings cowering in fear under an overhang on a rock ledge is false. The cave dwellers of southern France who began living there fifty thousand years ago did in fact live on rock ledges, but they also explored the dark caves in the cliff walls behind them. Using small sandstone oil lamps, which they invented and carried along in the palms of their hands, they penetrated up to a mile into the caves' interiors. There, by the light of their tiny lamps, they put their marks upon the cave walls in the form of signs and paintings.

I believe we are not content with what we already know and can do; we want action and growth—opportunities to explore our competence and mastery. I see the little girl in blue jeans in elementary school who rides her bicycle to the edge of her familiar territory, exploring the boundaries, all the way to the start of the streets with the big trees and the big houses, which she knows is alien country, shadowy, mysterious, forbidding. But the afternoon comes when she rides into it alone—rides through it and out the other side, triumphant. James A. Michener, the novelist, spoke for many of us when he said, "I like challenges. I don't mind defeat. I don't gloat over victories. I want to be in the ballgame."

Young or old, we want to be challenged. We want to shape, form, build our own lives. One of the most vivid events for parents is to hear their little child, scarcely a year and a half old, shout out the demand, "Me do it! Me do it myself!" Two-year-olds who take tests smile when they solve a difficult problem but go deadpan when they solve an easy one. Gifted children under-challenged in school are bored to the point of failure and may become disruptive in the classroom. When given more to do, they say, "The advanced work isn't hard stuff, it's fun." Specially designed cribs with motorized "mobiles" that move in response to an infant's head movement on a pressure-sensitive pillow evoke much smiling, cooing, and laughing when infants control the mobile themselves by moving their heads.

Judith Rodin and other psychologists who study aging find that growth and mastery are central to older people's sense of well-being. In experiments these researchers discovered that older men and women in nursing homes who were given some control over seemingly trivial aspects of their lives—taking care of a plant; choosing when to go to the movies; deciding what they would eat, how they would arrange their rooms, when they would talk on the telephone—felt more alert and happy than those without these choices.

Studies of job satisfaction, of which there are thousands, give convincing evidence that challenge and autonomy make work more satisfying. Unfortunately, in most jobs we can learn the skills in a few days; and after that, there is less room to move forward. Nonetheless, even if our work situation is confining, repetitive, boring, a prison of the mind, we create a way to grow. An assembly-line worker whose job was to tighten a set of screws all day long challenged himself for several years by experimenting with ways to shave a few seconds from his time.

Some people, for whom a dual life is possible, tolerate dull work by directing growth and mastery toward other goals. For example, Benedict Spinoza, the seventeenth-century Dutch philosopher, ground lenses while creating his philosophy; the nineteenth-century philosopher John Stuart Mill did correspondence for the East India Company and, on the side, wrote major works on economic and political theory; and, early in this century, Albert Einstein examined patent applications as he formed his theories of the universe.

People who cannot find growth and challenge in the workplace will search for special challenges and achievement elsewhere: losing weight, improving their bowling, mastering a six-iron shot on a downhill lie, making the perfect omelet, or seeking adventures. The "rich and nutty" adventures described in a magazine cover story called "Risking It All" included:

> rowing single-handed across the Pacific, climbing frozen water falls, skiing slopes too steep to stand on, exploring deep underwater caves, swimming twice around Manhattan, jumping off cliffs and buildings with parachutes, climbing skyscrapers, flying in fragile airplanes, sailing around the world single-handed.

Many of us who cannot climb, fly, jump, or sail (most of us, really) may turn to the simplest adventure of them all: experimenting with new foods and new products in the supermarket. The manufacturers respond to this interest by increasing the variety; each year brings twenty-five hundred new items. Probably no more than fifty basic items from a supermarket are needed for us to live well, but the supermarket display of thousands of items to choose from gives many people a sense of autonomy.

It appears, at first glance, that some lives are continually punctuated by winning and losing events; while others are quiet, with easy passage through the usual sequence of social roles in life, with no accidents and few surprises, and presumably little personality change. But when we look more carefully, it is clear that we generate our own wins and losses from the material we have to work with. One man said to me that you do not have to go to India to search for a simple and nonchallenging environment because the small New England town and the farming culture in which he grew up was like this. But then, on second thought, he realized that he had made winning and losing events out of nothing, objectively speaking. We are fated to make contests and set levels to strive for even when virtually none are imposed on us.

Somewhere between the conditions of slavery for the ancient Athenians in the stone quarries of Sicily, and the near omnipotence of Rameses, Attila the Hun, and Genghis Khan, we live our ordinary lives and seek to explore and master our part of the world.

HUMAN GOALS

In any large news and magazine store, the magazines are classified on shelves according to categories of interest that cover most of the range of human concerns: sports, homes, fame/celebrities, travel, money, hobbies (cars, stamps, photography, and so on), literature, politics, arts, fashion/style, food, gardening, sex, careers, movies, health, family, religion, and nature.

Within these categories, our ambitions get directed to some unusual ends. For example, Jesse Hart Rosdail, a fifty-nine-year-old fifth-grade teacher from Elmhurst, Illinois,

> spent two years trying to set foot on Tristan da Cunha, a windswept hunk of desolate volcanic rock in the middle of the South Atlantic. . . . In the past 39 years, according to the meticulous records which Rosdail keeps, he has journeyed 1,314,265 miles, and he regards himself as the world's champion globetrotter. The Guinness Book of World Records lists him in its Human Achievements section as the world's "Most Traveled Man."

And there are the creations of Isao Adachi:

> It is a small and beautiful world, the island of Japan revealed in the middle of the Bronx, in a greenhouse of a thousand chrysanthemums. Some are carefully shaped like waterfalls, others like miniature and ancient pine trees, still others like sailboats before the wind. The flowers bloom in ivory and in shades of red, yellow and purple. . . . Mr. Adachi, who is 36 years old, came here from Tokyo three years ago to bring the traditional Japanese chrysanthemum exhibition to the New York Botanical Garden in the Bronx. At last year's show, his second, many Japanese wept, explaining to startled garden staffers that Mr. Adachi's flowers, so exquisitely true to tradition, made them long for home.

Then there was the "ultimate marathon" in which "[a] thirty-two-year-old Australian, Peter Parcell, recently came through Christchurch, New Zealand, on his way around the world. Nothing too spectacular about this, except that Parcell is running around the globe."

Finally, we have Marsha Alexander's achievements in soup:

North Miami Beach, Fla.—It wasn't as momentous as the splitting of the atom, but the world should note that a contest to acclaim the best chicken soup was held the other day. No lives were lost. No governments fell. The sun also rose the next morning. . . . Magnanimous, willing to share her recipe (even a secret cooking tip), the winner, Marsha Alexander, took her triumph in stride. "You should taste my split-pea soup with flanken," she said. "Now that's a soup."

As for making money, Plato writing in the fourth century B.C. described those people who like to pile up a fortune instead of spending it: "The makers of fortunes have a second love of money as a creation of their own, resembling the affection of authors for their own poems, or of parents for their children, besides that natural love of it for the sake of use and profit."

A contemporary report comparing billionaires around the world elaborates on this point. Saudi Arabia's King Fahd, with perhaps $20 billion to dip into, has residences in London, the French Riviera, and Geneva. His new 500-foot yacht is the largest in the world and includes a 100-seat theater and a mosque. He has his choice of two 747's (his private planes). In contrast, Asian billionaires create but do not spend. ("They love the getting, not the spending.") The Tokyo executive of Japan's largest over-the-counter drug company "lives in an unpretentious house, walks to work, and eats a lunch of consommé, biscuits, and tea at his desk. . . . His wealth is $1.4 billion." The overseas Chinese "are probably the most frugal billionaires on earth when it comes to spending on themselves." For the founder of a plastics group who is worth $1.5 billion, "his idea of high living is to drink five beers with dinner before retiring at 9:00 P.M." He spends no money on himself, hates spending money on clothes, does not fly first class across the Pacific. A second—who is worth $2.5 billion, lives in an old two-story house, and wears an inexpensive Seiko watch, both of these acquired more than twenty years ago—says, "A simple life is more enjoyable."

COMPETITION AND SELFISHNESS

There are two basic ways of classifying human purposes—competitive versus cooperative, and selfish versus unselfish. Some people are made uneasy by thinking about winning and losing, and about ambition, almost as if they were taboo words from the world of selfish competition.

First, collectivists and egalitarians say that we should think not about winning and losing at all, but about "cooperation." This implies, mistakenly, that the notion of winning and losing applies only to competition between individuals or groups. In fact, we win or lose in our cooperative endeavors just as in our competitions. We must deal with achievement gaps in either case: the same psychological processes are used. We share goals with others and work together to reach them. A fire brigade works to save the children in a burning tenement. Teams of scientists from different nations cooperate to launch a space shuttle, to clean the atmosphere and the oceans, to control or eliminate a disease. We can succeed or we can fail in these tasks. If we win, we all win; if we lose, we all lose.

Consider children's games. With their origins lost in the obscurity of prehistory, cooperative games occur in almost all societies, side by side with competitive games. In cooperative games, the children play to overcome challenges, not to overcome other people. In the traditional game "King of the Mountain," the rules may say that only one person should be king and all the others shoved down the hill; but the rules are reversed in the cooperative game: the goal is to get as many as possible to the top, and the children work together to achieve this.

We may use competitive or cooperative actions as we choose or as social rules dictate. What we decide will vary from one event to another. Winning does not require that we be against someone else; we can reach our goals through competition or cooperation. Winning is not just the result of selfish individualism. Ours is not a world in which the price of one person's happiness is someone else's unhappiness. Many have a vision of a world in which individuals achieve happiness by cooperating with others to increase the happiness of all, rather than by winning at others' expense and lessening their happiness.

Second, in earlier times and to some extent today, a drive for ambition is associated with selfish purposes. In early Roman days, *ambition* had the connotation of greediness and selfishness, and of being individualistic and competitive. The word comes from the Latin *ambit,* meaning "to go around," and was used later to describe Roman politicians going around and hustling votes. Two thousand years later, in the early 1900s, a poet still could write:

> *I had Ambition, by which sin*
> *The angels fell;*
> *I climbed and, step by step, O Lord,*
> *Ascended into Hell.*

Over the centuries, though, the evil overtones have given way to distinction between good and bad ambitions. The novelist Joseph Conrad wrote that all ambitions are acceptable except "those that climb upward on the miseries or credulities of mankind." Shakespeare wrote of one who was "chok'd with ambition of the meaner sort," in comparison with a benign type. In present times, *ambition* may suggest equally a praiseworthy or a base desire; the concept is morally neutral. It is what we seek, not the basic drive itself, that involves moral issues.

Even though ambition in the service of altruism may seem contradictory, Albert Schweitzer certainly had a powerful ambition to do good when in the 1930s he left behind his career as musician and theologian and established the little hospital in the jungle in Lambaréné, Africa. And similarly for the social worker Jane Addams who in 1889 established in Chicago the first settlement house for the poor; for the volunteers in the International Red Cross in the Second World War who cared for the casualties; for the workers in the United Nations Children's Fund (UNICEF) who aid the starving children of the world; and for Mother Teresa who today assists the sick and poor in Calcutta. Are we supposed to think that these persons were less driven toward their goals than are "selfish individualists"?

In sum, in this book I use the word *ambition* in a broader sense to refer to the basic human drive for growth and mastery. Whether in competitive or cooperative form, or selfish or selfless, it is the general desire to achieve as it is expressed in daily life.

CULTURE AND HISTORY

From earliest times, humans have described differences among tribes or countries or nations—differences in how they see the world, how they think, how they know. Myths are created about the Garden of Eden, about the Orient, about the Earth Mother, myths about places and heroic figures free of ambition and passion, of winning and losing.

Research in anthropology is rich in descriptions of how cultures differ in their valued goals and in their conceptions of the desirable adult personality. The dimensions include an emphasis on orderliness versus spontaneity, on vengeance and aggression versus harmony, on future versus present orientation, on individualism versus social conformity.

For nearly one hundred and fifty years, observers have described America as individualistic and achievement-oriented, with a high value placed on success. No matter how much Americans have, they want more. It is said that America is the country where people come to fulfill their personal dreams, where they can express their competitive and entrepreneurial spirit. Our language has elaborated on this part of human nature and these kinds of life experience. Eskimos have many terms for different kinds of snow, and Tibetans have many terms for different states of being, but we have many words related to becoming wealthy and successful in work careers.

Janet T. Spence in her 1986 presidential address to the American Psychological Association said, "The United States is an achievement-oriented society that has historically encouraged and honored individual accomplishment and the attainment of material prosperity." True enough. But what is distinctive about the United States is not that it is "achievement-oriented," but that it values individual accomplishment and material prosperity.

We must not equate the drive for growth and mastery with capitalism, free enterprise, and the "Protestant ethic." The important point is that every nation or culture is "achievement-oriented" toward its own characteristic goals.

Either individualism or collectivism is chosen by the cultures of the world. Certain societies value individual development and independence; others value loyalty to the in group and harmonious interpersonal relations. The Japanese place more value on predictable behavior, stability, and personal relationships than on social mobility and individual freedom, but pursue these goals just as intensely as Americans pursue their own.

The universality of ambition is masked by differences in individual goals and in cultural theories of human character. These theories are created, probably, to fit the basic economic and social system of each nation. The theory that humans are acquisitive and competitive goes along with Western capitalism. Western civilization's conception of humans involves supreme development of an individual's talent, a star system, as expressed by the novelist Ayn Rand in *Atlas Shrugged* (1957). The view that humans are cooperative and concerned with group rather than individual achievements sometimes is linked with the emergence of socialism and communism as forms of society. In the People's Republic of China, the Confucian classics that have been used for hundreds of years to teach youngsters about human nature—such as "Men at their birth are naturally good"—are being analyzed and corrected to fit the contemporary Chinese social order.

The images of human nature in our own and other societies are mainly ideals and ideologies, rather than accurate descriptions of national character. They do not account for what really goes on. It is as if we took the Ten Commandments from Christianity as true descriptions of human conduct. I believe that as we get away from these "texts" about idealized human nature for a particular society—a kind of scripture reading—and move on to observable behavior, we get much closer to the elements of the universal character of humans. There is intense competition in seminaries, and among ministers of all faiths, to get ahead while doing good. A top college football player, trying to decide between becoming a professional football player or entering the priesthood, says he could compete just as well in either sector of life.

There is a proverb from Epicurus, writing in the third century B.C., "Do not spoil what you have by desiring what you have not; but remember that what you now have was once among things only hoped for." This may sound like wise advice, but it appears to be a psychological impossibility. It is more the nature of humans to desire what they do not have, with their aspirations expanding to the limits of what they believe is their controllable environment. In fact, it is likely that Epicurus and other Greek philosophers prescribing moderation did not actually describe contemporary Greek culture. Instead, they meant to be helpful in an intensely competitive society.

Although it is generally believed that most Eastern religions eliminate ambition, the same gap between the prescribed ideal and real behavior exists in the East as in the West. The deviations in real life from religious doctrine show striving, growing, wanting, winning, or losing. The fact is that Asian societies are shot through with ambition, although expressed in non-Western ways. When Buddhism promises to show you how to achieve enlightenment, *achieve* is the key word.

Some people seek perfection in withdrawal, their ambition to be drained of worldly desire. But, in order to achieve this state, one must work hard and strive and achieve. Although a person may say, "I aspire to do nothing," the person is not necessarily doing nothing. Even the fact that the way to achieve it is to practice not achieving should not hide the truth. The practice of not achieving is itself an achievement effort; and one can win or lose—that is, reach or not reach this goal—in the same way that one can in playing tennis or investing in a stock. In the ashrams in India, Harvard dropouts as well as Indians in the early stages of their instruction are striving to rise rapidly toward the loss of self, competing to see who gets there fastest, who is the best student of the guru teaching selflessness. Ankle deep in the mud of the streets of Calcutta, young men in orange robes beg to learn humility. Back at the ashram in the evening, they compare who got the most alms during the day, and then look for approval for having expressed their ambition to be selfless. In the later stages of their training, they strive, but do not compete with each other. They see the possibility that, after they are firmly established in their own path, they may reach the desired end. But they still are intensely motivated to master the penance, the absolution, the self-imposed mental and physical torment to reach the desired ultimate state.

To the question whether humans were always like this, the best answer seems to be yes. The psychiatrist-researcher David A. Hamburg, president of the Carnegie Corporation, writes that primates appeared early among the mammals and have been present for at least fifty million years:

> The biological equipment of the human organism is mostly very old. In addition to obvious physical characteristics, some of our emotional responses, tendencies and learning orientations are probably a part of that biological equipment, built into the organism because they worked well in adaptation over many thousands, and even millions, of years.

I believe that we make the same mistake in our assumptions about differences in historical periods that we make about cultural differences. We believe that there were times in history when people did not work hard and were carefree about the future. We mistake historical changes in our goals with changes in basic human nature. We change what we want in life, but history does not change the human animal. Each generation lives according to its own customs. The goals that are set, and the levels of achievement that are realistic to strive for, are affected by the events and characteristics of a particular historical period, such as economic changes, religious beliefs, prejudices, plagues, and wars. In Western civilization during several centuries, the pursuit of material and worldly goals of wealth and property replaced the pursuit of personal salvation through the church. Still, the intensity with which both sets of goals were striven for—after all, we killed for both—and the methods of our dealing with winning or losing along the way stayed the same. To say that the importance of achievement waxes and wanes across historical times is only to confuse "achievement" with the specific and varying desires for wealth and property and career success. Humanity striving at the level of just manageable difficulty is timeless; what it strives toward changes from era to era.

Consider these alleged changes in American youth during the past three decades: In the 1980s, one magazine said, "The official cheer of 1984: 'Go for it!'" A new book was entitled *Go For It! How to Win at Love, Work, and Play.* Miles Laboratory changed the slogan for Alka-Seltzer from the usual concern about overeating to the more contemporary: "For the symptoms of stress that come with success." Business edged out sex and real estate as the topic of the 1980s. *Esquire* described the decade "as a time of boundless ambition. People are consumed by a desire to acquire more of everything." An advertisement in *Fortune* said, "Nobody's going to hand you success on a silver platter. If you want to make it, you'll have to make it on your own. Your own drive, your own guts, your own energy, your own ambition. Yes, ambition. You don't have to hide it anymore. Society's decided that now it's OK to be up-front about the drive for success."

The fact is that to be "very well-off financially" was a goal of 75 percent of American college freshmen in 1985, but of just 45 percent in 1967. This increase in the pursuit of wealth was at the expense of the goal to "develop a meaningful philosophy of life," which declined from 82 percent to 42 percent during this same era. In the 1960s and 1970s, young people wanted self-actualization and self-fulfillment in contributing to the greater good of their society. Nevertheless, these intrinsic, benign, non-materialistic goals were sought after with an intensity no different from the pursuit of money, fame, and power in the 1980s. Even some of the alternative-culture communities—the ashrams, the flower-child communes—competed with each other to be the best of the cooperative, noncompetitive little societies. These changes in goals do not indicate any change in basic human nature or in fundamental processes for dealing with achievement gaps.

While looking for alternative images of human nature, I started with the world literature on utopias and the science fiction of the past hundred years. My assumption was that our human evolution is not over—that nature is not finished with us—and that we should see what these authors believe lies ahead.

The main theme in this body of work is how scientific discoveries affect our social institutions. The authors are less creative where changes in human nature are concerned. Some experiment with the idea of changes, writing about sex becoming irrelevant to reproduction, and aggression fading away through negative selection in the species. But the basic growth and mastery character of humans remains unchanged. Even when humans in science fiction have spread throughout the galaxies, and lost colonies evolve into quite different forms of life, where they may become cold-blooded, shape-changing humans, they still keep this basic element of character. And, if robots—which are genetically and psychologically engineered to a variety of specifications and used or sold to other species throughout the galaxies—are supposed to be as close to humans as possible, then they are created to retain the fundamental drive.

The fact is that there is no great work on "changed personalities" in the utopian or science fiction literature. The authors do not imagine a different human nature, without ambition. In fact, the stories that describe attempts to control this nature and to change it (Aldous Huxley's *Brave New World* [1932] and Ray Bradbury's *Fahrenheit 451* [1953] are the most famous of these) have a hero or heroine who challenges the system and leads the breakout and re-creation of a society that allows expression of growth and mastery.

WOMEN AND MEN

Social custom may channel the interests of men and women into different sectors of life, where they win and lose in different kinds of venture. But everything in the process of dealing with achievement gaps is similar: the dreams, the motivation, the management of winning and losing, the creation of new goals.

Some women say, "I don't see the world in terms of success or failure, or of winning and losing"; but, rather, "We are not in the picture—it doesn't fit us." I believe this is simply a matter of framing things differently, a matter of language and what we choose to call achievement. In the traditional male and female roles, a man piling up and defending his money is no more intense than a mother raising and defending her children. Women's aspirations are as high, and the wish to achieve as powerful in creating close and supportive interpersonal relationships, as men's are in creating occupational careers.

A traditional male may say he wants to concentrate on career achievement and not sacrifice it to friendships and family. But a woman in the traditional family role says that she will not sacrifice her achievements in the interpersonal and family realms just to achieve in her career. There is no reason to believe that the man's ambition is more powerful than the woman's. Moreover, we can easily imagine a society in which the activities concerned with intimacy and affiliation were held to be of highest importance, and strivings to succeed in this sector were called achievement-oriented; in contrast, the activities in the work role would be viewed as unimportant, something that has to be done in order to live, but not as a sector in which one strives to excel.

Where losing and winning are concerned, in situations defined as equally competitive for both boys and girls, there are no differences in achievement striving. Hundreds of experiments show no gender differences in levels of aspiration. It is only in stereo-typed, role-defined activities that differences appear: boys' attainment standards are higher in athletic and mechanical skills; and girls' standards are higher in artistic, verbal, and social skills.

Research has established that young males are more aggressive than females. Early in childhood, boys and girls have different types of play. Boys are rougher, with more loud shouting: "On wheeled vehicles boys (3 to 5) play ramming games while girls ride around and try not to bump into each other." Still both are trying; they only have different goals. What all this research shows is that there are differences in what men and women emphasize in their lives, but not in how hard they strive or in how they deal with winning and losing.

When women get into what have been traditionally male roles, they are as competitive and concerned about winning and losing as men are in these activities. Research shows that women, when in the role of executive, are more like executive men than they are different, in terms of goals, motives, personalities, and behavior.

The Center for Creative Leadership summarizes this research and points out:

> Over the years, many people have argued that the abilities and attitudes of male managers are very different from those of female managers. Historically, the perceived differences have been used to keep women out of management, but now it has become fashionable to say that the differences are beneficial, that women will complement men in the management ranks and bring a healthy balance to business.

As it turns out, the data show that these alleged gender differences are not there in the workplace. Research has revealed that executive women are not more impulsive, not better able to reduce interpersonal friction, not more understanding or humanitarian, not less dominant, not less optimistic about success, and not less able to define and attain goals than men.

Research on men describes how in midlife they become more interested in intimacy and nurturance. This change may occur because they are starting to top out in their careers and thus to move their interests and energies into different sectors of life where they can find challenges—in many instances, their families and their interpersonal relationships. One man said to me, "I see now that it was not until I was forty-two years old that I was willing to say that I would die for my wife and children."

But it is also true that after children have been born and raised, with men and women having made their separate contributions, the social pressures to maintain the strongly differentiated gender roles taught to men in earlier years are lifted. They are free to move back toward the center of a common humanity, where concerns with intimacy, affiliations, and nurturance are mixed with self-assertions and independence for both men and women.

INDIVIDUAL DIFFERENCES

We believe that we are different from everyone else in certain ways; that our inherited genes and unusual life experiences interact to produce our unique personalities.

This belief is sometimes weakened by extraordinary experiences. During the Second World War in Sweden, babies and young children were moved from the cities to the country to protect them from the dangers of the war. They grew up in foster homes. Among these children were about 1,600 pairs of identical twins—twins who were exactly the same in their biological genetic inheritance. Several years ago, the official records of the movement of these children were found in government archives. It turned out that among the pairs of identical twins there were about 150 pairs in which the men and women involved—now about forty to fifty years old—did not know that they had an identical twin. It was a major shock to their sense of their own uniqueness to learn that there was another human born exactly like them—like finding a parallel universe where another "you" exists. Naturally, these twins were intensely curious to meet their twin and see what that other brother or sister had accomplished in his or her life, using exactly the same material to start with, and to see how different or not either had become.

In wartime an enemy may set out to weaken or destroy a prisoner's sense of identity by a process referred to as "identity stripping" and "de-individuation." Methods include removing all personal possessions; clothing people in uniforms or forcing them to be naked, masked, or disguised in other ways; and prohibiting speech and writing. It is not the loss of freedom or the torture that is most damaging; it is the destruction of the person's sense of uniqueness.

But how different are we, really? The science of genetics tells us that each person is unique—except for identical twins—in the history of the human species and always will be. There never has been nor ever will be another person with one's genetic characteristics. But the newest research shows that individual differences in human genes are small. This genetic uniqueness of individuals occurs within such a small range that, in many respects, people are more alike than different.

There is a Museum of Smells that presents the fifty best-known odors. Over 95 percent of Americans can identify Ivory Soap, Coca-Cola, coffee, and other familiar substances. Thus, we are essentially alike in how the different odors register in our minds. This is also the case for the taste of different foods (otherwise, chefs in big restaurants could not be sure that they were preparing dishes that would please the public). It turns out that most personal interests that we believe are unusual are not. A "Look Like Groucho Contest" in Boston in the 1980s brought out one thousand imitators of Groucho Marx. In Heidelberg, Germany, a professor plants his yard with yews, an apple tree, variegated euonymus, forsythia, lilacs, roses, a Japanese maple, Mugho pines, birches, and flowers—but it is the same as the garden of the professor in Princeton. And so it is with other experiences: cold-water swimming, the aerobic effect of running, sexual intercourse, lying on a beach in the hot sun, viewing a sunset. We like to think that our reactions to a taste or a sunset or another person are unique, and believe that they cannot be shared—except by our poets. The truth is most of us experience these events in much the same ways.

As for personalities, we all have seen people with intense energy whose motors are always running, always testing their limits, working near 100-percent capacity, who always play to win (even in a game with a child). Other people seem lazy, timid, fearful of trying, content to idle away the days. Still others are rigid and resist anything new, determined to stay the same regardless of any experience. Their opposites seem mercurial in character, shifting from week to week, always trying something new. Brilliant analytical minds concentrate on diagnosing the nature of a problem, sorting out means and ends, setting priorities for actions to be taken; while other, unfortunate fellow humans cannot think clearly because of biological or psychological damage. These extremes of human personality make interesting case studies and are the starting point for scientific research on personality varieties.

How different we are from one another, and how differences affect our actions, are long-debated issues among scholars. Like genetic endowment, the variation in human personalities may turn out to be small. We might be surprised to find out that under all our differences we are much more similar than we like to believe. How we direct our ambitions varies according to our individual natures, our gender, our culture, our time in history;

but behind this is the universal drive for growth and mastery.

There is this one exception: that class of human wreckage, those people overcome by events or disabilities that are totally beyond an individual's power to ameliorate. Many become permanently different from other human beings. Unable to manage the event or to escape reality by burying it in the unconscious, they must live with a situation for which there is no solution—a situation that kills many human spirits, extinguishing the drive for growth and mastery. Still, such unfortunate people have their dreams, however little they may be expressed in terms of ordinary social definitions of purpose, or even expressed at all. Charlie Smith has written of the gravely injured:

> "You think that I sit in this wheelchair dreaming of the time when I could dance," they cried, "but you're wrong; I sit here dreaming that I could leap up and strangle you." . . . I love the stories about the quadriplegic begging for someone to smother him, praying twenty-four hours a day for thugs to come and kill his parents so that the doctors would turn off the goddamn machinery keeping him alive.

Some men and women survive potential inner death by finding extraordinary resources to express their need for growth. We need to seek out in unusual places the dreams of such broken lives. Almost always we will find something.

2

Looking for Just Manageable Difficulties

The drive for growth and mastery is, though powerful, curiously bounded. We choose challenges that are difficult enough to perplex and test our powers yet not so tough that we are likely to face severe or frequent failure. Most of the time we try to arrange things so that we are neither pushed to the limit nor coasting, neither overloaded nor underloaded. We seek a level of effort that the psychologist Nicholas Hobbs called the level of "just manageable difficulty":

> We sometimes think of the well-adjusted person as having very few problems, while, in fact, just the opposite is true. When a person is ill or injured or crushed with grief or deeply frightened, the range of his concerns become sharply constricted; his problems diminish in scope and quality and complexity.
>
> By contrast, the healthy person, the person healthy in body and mind and spirit, is a person with many difficulties. He has a lot of problems, many of which he has deliberately chosen with the sure knowledge that in working toward their solution, he will become more the person he would like to be.

Part of the art of choosing difficulties is to select those that are indeed just manageable. If the difficulties chosen are too easy, life is boring; if they are too hard, life is defeating.

This level of manageable difficulty is not some "set-point" to which we always return after a deviation, like a set-point in human physiology such as the amount of salt in our blood. Our point of psychological equilibrium keeps changing.

THE PROBLEM WITH WINNING

We all know that failure must be dealt with, but we are less likely to understand that winning brings its problems, too. Winning requires management just as surely as does losing. Wins and losses both demand that we set a new level of difficulty, but they are not just mirror images of each other. If we do not find a new challenge after winning, we are bored, apathetic, unhappy. Probably all of us would rather have to adjust to winning than to losing; only a fool would say otherwise. Nevertheless, winning big is as hard to manage as a big loss.

Some people will say, "Losing hurts more than winning feels good." Research in psychology supports this observation. We adapt to winning more rapidly than we do to losing. We raise our sights and move ahead quickly from a win, and recover more slowly from a loss. Experiments in psychology laboratories show that losing is more painful than winning is pleasurable. Losing hurts even more if you feel you should have won than if you did your best against overwhelming odds.

However, time reduces the pain of losing. A sign on the counter of an automobile repair service shop says, "The memory of poor quality lasts longer than the sweetness of low price." Catchy, but not true. Bad events tend to disappear from memory, to be suppressed or repressed. This conclusion comes from fifty years of experiments on memory, such as the following: college students were asked to list events from the preceding summer that were good and bad; six months later, they had forgotten more of the bad than the good events.

In the actual management of our achievement gaps, as I have noted, we change some elements of our actions. If we fail, we cut back by decreasing the degree of difficulty. This may mean searching for new behavior that works better, extending our timetable for achieving a particular goal, or reducing the amount or quality we expect to get. If none of these strategies works, we will, in the end, give up this goal.

Winning sets a different process in motion. When we win, the response is to increase the degree of difficulty. We set a shorter timetable for the next endeavor, raising expectations of how much we can achieve, even broadening out and adding new goals. We will try to get there earlier or faster, and to get more or better. If running on the beach, we may try to go all the way to the lighthouse this time (an extra mile) and pick up speed at the same time. If swimming in the ocean, we may swim directly out a half-mile (instead of a usual quarter-mile), until struck by the sudden realization "I don't belong here"; or, we might try to do the crawl by breathing on the left side, doing it the harder way. Sometimes when winning is no fun because it is too easy, we will handicap ourselves to make an action interesting to us. In sports, when playing against a weaker opponent, we will give away strokes or points. In other situations, we may increase the difficulty by trying the same task without any help, without a tool, with the opposite hand, or with one hand tied behind our back.

Winning raises our hopes; losing lowers them. As Tocqueville wrote about democracy in the United States when it was a new nation, social movements are not caused by failure and frustration but spring from rising strength. And so it is today. Recently at Howard University, the leading primarily black university in the United States, students escalated a demonstration after achieving their goal of forcing the resignation of the Republican Party chairman, Lee Atwater, from the college's board of trustees. The protesters went on to disrupt classes and demand assurances of financial aid and improved campus housing. It is when inequality declines that aspirations rise and rebellions occur. T. George Harris, former editor of *Psychology Today,* spoke of this to me as "the snake of hope"; prison riots, he notes, start when the food is getting better, not worse.

There are broad implications here for what happens to people when they are successful at work. Once you get good at a particular job, it no longer takes most of your ability to do it well. So you set your sights higher and push on to more demanding work. Ongoing studies of American Telephone & Telegraph executives show that those who were successful in reaching the middle-management level after eight years gradually became more work-oriented. The less successful men, by contrast, focused their energies more on their families and their religious, recreational, and social activities.

But here's the hitch. People can become psychologically trapped by their own success as they race to keep up with the rising expectations bred by each new achievement. With each success, they raise their level of difficulty, climbing up a ladder of subgoals, moving faster, raising aspirations, and at some point reaching the limit of their capacity.

At this point, successful performance becomes difficult, and we begin to lose more often than we win. Our resources are squeezed to the utmost, and the climb has ended. The business executive, promoted beyond a level of just manageable difficulty, ends up being held together by a thin paste of alcohol, saunas, and antibiotics, unable to escape the daily challenge of the job. The familiar "Peter Principle" operates: the executive has risen to his or her personal level of incompetence.

FINDING THE RIGHT LEVEL

Where is the right level of difficulty? We can define it to ourselves, subjectively, and tell others when we are there or when life is too easy or too hard. But objectively, who can say? There are three clues to what may be going on. One way to describe a level of difficulty is in terms of the probability that our action will succeed or fail. Research on artificial tasks shows that we are most strongly motivated to try to achieve success when we know the risk of failure to be about fifty-fifty. The joy of winning is enhanced by the threat of failure. Activities that involve no risk cannot provide the joy of achievement. But this research is in the

laboratory. If in real life we were to wait for fifty-fifty odds in setting our levels of action, we would lose as often as we win. I do
not believe that is true for most of our lives—although as far as I
know, no one has studied the actual odds.

Some economists say that nine out of ten new small businesses
will fail. In a television broadcast of the Kentucky Derby, the
sportscaster Jim McKay said, as I recall, "This is a sport where
everyone loses a lot more often than they win." But what goes on
in small businesses and horse racing does not necessarily happen
in other sectors of life. Do our purposeful activities in our families, health, recreation, and careers fail more often than they succeed? No one seems to have counted.

I believe that in everyday life we expect to win or we would not
act, but we do not seek to maximize the probability of success to
the point where we are nearly certain of an outcome before we
begin. Our chances of winning change from time to time and
from one situation to another—being sometimes fifty-fifty or less
but, I think, usually more.

A long tradition of research in psychology confirms common-
sense beliefs about the relationship between risk and reward. If
we want something very much, we are willing to take more of a
chance—a long shot—to get it. Thus, the chances of losing usually will be greater in situations where we place a very high value
on our goal. It follows that a given person will have different risk
levels for various situations, depending on how much one values
success in them. One person will be more risk-oriented in love
affairs but less so in purely monetary matters. Another person
will be just the opposite.

Here is another approach to identifying the level of just manageable difficulty. The economist H. F. Clark has reported that
no matter what level of income Americans reach, we want, on
the average, about 25 percent more. When we have that, we want
another 25 percent. People in all social classes, regardless of their
income, set goals for about 25 percent more than they have.
Research in economics shows that when we get tax cuts, we put
more into savings at first but gradually increase our spending.
We react the same way to wage increases: instead of putting
money away in savings, we spend it. Riches enlarge rather than

satisfy appetites. The boat owner steps up in 25-percent jumps from a 15-footer to a 19-footer, from there to a 25-footer, and so on up to the ocean-going yacht (with names to go with them— *Last Dollar, Over the Edge,* and, ironically, *Pocket Change*). And if we had a measuring rod for fame or good works or love, the 25-percent rule still might apply.

The third and best way to get at the meaning of levels of just manageable difficulty is to consider the relationship between the effort we put into the performance of a particular task and our actual capacity to do it—our "performance/capacity ratio." In some situations, one may have an easy time, drawing little on one's capacity. At other times, one draws on one's reserves, pushing oneself to the limit. If one is expending a lot of effort in one sector of life over a long period—in a situation demanding a high performance/capacity ratio—one is likely to ease up in some other area of life during the same span.

Despite the many similarities among people, individuals differ in the performance/capacity ratio with which they feel comfortable. I cannot say what the exact ratio might be in a given case, but I would estimate that something close to 80 percent is the standard ratio for most of us, averaged across events. (Or is it 60 percent? Perhaps we always have more in reserve than we know is there.)

I should make the point, I think, that this performance/capacity ratio is not tied to the riskiness of a venture. One may be required to work very hard (or very lightly) on enterprises whether or not one has a high probability of succeeding: that is, one may know one will be successful, but it will take a lot of hard work.

Working harder raises one's performance/capacity ratio. Of course, if one has been taking it easy for a while, then one may only come back up to one's usual level of effort. More likely, one applies a short burst of higher-than-normal intensity. If one succeeds and the event has passed, then one can rest. However, if one must stay at this excessive level of effort, one thinks, "If this keeps up, I'm going to have to quit or make some changes or leave." One must take the extra energy used here from some other sector of life.

How hard one is working obviously varies from time to time.

Life has plenty of hundred-yard dashes, but many slow walks, too. Brief respites from the usual striving and scrambling—periods when some tasks require little effort—offer a welcome change of pace. I know of men who have changed careers when, in fact, they only needed three weeks off. There are "time-out" periods during the day or the week when we are resting, not striving. A Roper Poll lists some activities that people say they look forward to in an average day: watching television, checking the mail, taking a shower or bath, spending time on a hobby, getting in the house once day is over, taking a break during work, reading the morning newspaper, cooking dinner.

These are routine satisfactions, the slow walks that balance the hundred-yard dashes. Many of them are physical pleasures rather than achievements involving wins and losses. If they are disrupted—the TV set does not work, the mail does not come, the hot water heater does not work—we would hardly call these losses or failures involving ambition. The lack of television is hardly a loss in the sense I have been describing.

Time-out periods last only so long, though, and then we want to get back in action. Even in our daily activities, the drive for growth shows itself: we hunt for a better TV show, try to read the newspaper faster, plan a gourmet dinner, attempt to do something more challenging in our hobby. And on vacation, after a while we get restless and want to go back to work.

BELIEFS ABOUT OUR CAPACITIES

We set our levels of effort to accord with our beliefs about our capacities—how intelligent, strong, healthy, vigorous, wealthy, creative, physically attractive, sexually virile, and so on, we think we are. For example, one friend who, though slight in stature and subject to attacks of flu, has intense desires of many kinds, describes himself as a Rolls-Royce engine in a V-8 chassis. He is aware that his physical strength will not support the burden of his strong ambitions.

Although we have some general beliefs about our capacities, those beliefs are usually specific to a given characteristic.

Children seem to have fantasies of being able to do anything, but research shows they make specific distinctions between, say, being good at schoolwork, making friends, playing all kinds of sports, and having good looks. The biographer Arthur Mizener quotes the novelist F. Scott Fitzgerald taking stock of his assets: "'I didn't have the two top things—great animal magnetism or money,' he once said of himself, 'I have the two second things, though—good looks and intelligence, so I always got the top girl. . . .' He seemed to look on the task of winning them as a competition. It excited him."

Built into us as humans is the need to find out how we stand with regard to our abilities. We evaluate our resources as we assess our chances of success. Life from birth onward is a continuous self testing to find out what we can do. During its waking hours, the infant actively explores its abilities to deal with the environment: it grasps, it moves parts of its tiny body, seeing what happens. Children's beliefs about their capacities, the sense that "I can do this"—draw a dog, lift a stone, climb a bookcase, ride a bike—grow and become more differentiated. Later, teenagers explore the limits of the possible, testing just what they can do as their capacities increase with age. In adulthood, new qualities need to be appraised because the tasks are different. We may need to test the truth about our integrity, judgment, the accuracy of our knowledge, our capacity for self-control.

Consider the widespread personal interest in test scores of intelligence. People pay to be tested, whether or not any organization demands it. Even though the familiar SSAT's and SAT's are being dropped by private secondary schools, colleges, and universities as a basis for admission, the tests continue to be sold to individuals because of their enduring curiosity about intellectual capacity.

Fewer of us have any feedback from tests of our personality characteristics. Our beliefs about our social talents or our leadership abilities are sometimes distorted by our wishes about how we want to be. But when a standardized test gives us a profile of where we rank on a dozen or so personality characteristics, it can bring an abrupt change in our beliefs.

We do not test and evaluate all our abilities; only some are relevant to our goals. Today intelligence is valued as a means to many ends; but once upon a time, courage and skill in arms were prized. On the frontier, it was strength and bravery that counted. Among the early Christians, it was the ability to endure criticism, calumny, and even death. There are many things we will never know about ourselves, and our curiosity spills over into imagining how we might act in situations we will never experience.

Certainly our experiences have contributed to substantial differences among us in the number and accuracy of our beliefs about our capacities. Some of us hold beliefs that are relatively untested, and have gone through life more or less protected from challenge; others have had much reality testing. Sometimes we learn directly from confrontation with nature or with a task—a small, bright dagger of self-insight. Although the novelist John Barth writes, "Self-insight is always bad news," I think this applies more to our desires than to our capacities. Understanding the latter is almost always good news because it feeds into rational action. Albert Einstein, for example, explained his choice of physics, not mathematics, as his field of study:

> This was obviously due to the fact that my intuition was not strong enough in the field of mathematics in order to differentiate clearly the fundamentally important, that which is really basic, from the rest of the more or less dispensable erudition. In this field [physics], however, I soon learned to scent out that which was able to lead to fundamentals and to turn aside from everything else, from the multitude of things which clutter up the mind and divert it from the essentials.

Some of what we believe about our capacities is wrong. We make significant errors even about characteristics such as intelligence, where we might expect that we had been tested often by reality. Our belief that we are dumb, smart, or average comes from what our parents and brothers and sisters have told us, from our grades in school, intelligence test scores, work successes, and puzzle-solving experiences. Nevertheless, research on self-ratings of intelligence, when compared with intelligence test scores, reveals big errors of overestimation and underestimation.

A survey of 10,000 public and private school students in the ninth through the twelfth grades asked, "How would you say you compare in intelligence with other high school students in the United States?" The six possible answers ranged from "I am definitely below average in intelligence" to "I am among the highest in intelligence." In the public schools, of the 1,500 students scoring in the lowest ranks on intelligence tests, 175 believed they actually were among the highest, and another 250 believed they were above average. At the other end, among the 1,500 boys and girls in the top 30 percent in actual intelligence test scores, 300 rated themselves as below average or only average.

The college plans of these students in grades nine to twelve were based on their self-judgments. The higher they rated their intelligence, the more likely they were to hope for a college education. (This relationship holds up even when the students were matched on other factors that might affect going to college, such as parents' educational background and the students' actual measured intelligence.) Thus, the some 15 percent of American youth who overestimate or underestimate their capacities have plans that are either too grand or too humble relative to their true capacities.

The psychologist Deborah Phillips has made similar studies of third, fifth, and ninth-grade students, concentrating on those who underestimate their actual abilities. Approximately 20 percent had beliefs about themselves that were significant underestimates (what she calls the "illusion of incompetence").

Why should we have these mistaken beliefs about ourselves? First, although we usually want to know as much as we can about our abilities, in fact there are occasions when the information hurts. Rather than deal with the knowledge and change our plans for achievement accordingly, we sometimes try to screen it out and hide from it as long as possible. As a result, some of our beliefs about our capacities are unconscious and have never been examined critically. Although experience may bring some to awareness, others lie too deep to surface in this way. A major objective of psychodynamic psychotherapy is to bring these beliefs to consciousness so that they can be examined objectively and checked against reality.

Second, although we sometimes underrate our capacities,

most often we overestimate. Ninety-five percent of American men, for example, estimate that they are in the top 50 percent in social skills. National surveys report that we feel about nine years younger than we really are, and that we believe we look about five years younger than we are. Some psychologists describe this as denial or repression, assuming that we do know our capacities, but that we inflate our estimates to gain self-respect. Another explanation is that optimism is a human characteristic (as I will discuss in chapter 4), a built-in inflation factor that says, "I am better than they think," and is linked with the drive for growth and mastery.

Third, we may be ignorant about what we can do because we have never tried many things and thus have no data from life experience. We may think we can do something, but really are more able or less able than we think. Fourth, we may be wrong because our capacities have changed. When we are young and growing up, we are getting stronger and smarter and gaining skills. At the other end of the life span, the general biomedical decline, along with injuries that are slow to be repaired, reduce our power.

The errors we make are larger and more frequent when the facts are soft and ambiguous. The self-ratings of sixth-grade children on their physical attractiveness are not at all related to the ratings given by their teachers. Studies of eighth-grade children show that they evaluate their own popularity less accurately than they do their academic and athletic capacity and performance.

Because even the scientific measures of various capacities and personality characteristics are themselves imperfect, in the end we still must face the question of how much faith we should have in ourselves. We can stand apart from ourselves and analyze our beliefs about our capacities. We can think about why we think the way we do—the way we get confused. We can have knowledge about our knowledge—about how little we know. We have emotions about our emotions, as when we are ashamed of being shy, or get angry because of having gotten angry. We have motives about our motives, as when we want to overcome the desire for food, drink, or another person. In the same way, we can think about our beliefs about capacities. We might respond by saying yes to the personality test item "I seldom have any doubts about my abilities; I know my strengths and I know my weaknesses," and even say, "There isn't much a psychiatrist could tell me about myself that I don't already know." But other people will agree with "I often wonder what kind of person I really am."

Is it foolish to believe we can achieve a particular goal without some firm basis for the belief? When should one throw in the towel? What is courage in this sense? When we see people who persist in the face of contrary evidence and succeed, we think of them as heroes overcoming impossible obstacles. But when one of them fails, we think of that person as headstrong, foolhardy, and bent on self-destruction. A person who loses an arm in an accident, or regains sight in middle age after twenty years of blindness, readily alters a whole body of beliefs about personal competence, power, attractiveness, and the rest. In ordinary life, such rapid change is not so easy.

The lack of precision in standard tests of capacities and the likelihood, if not almost certainty, that our abilities are not correctly assessed by our contemporaries, means that most of us must and do make up our own minds. In setting our levels of difficulty, we cannot be sure of how much or how little we can do. We can use what facts we have; and beyond this, life is a gamble—an adventure in winning and losing.

UNDERLOADS AND OVERLOADS

Society generally forms an opinion about the capacities of people and sets standards for what should be expected in different situations. These social norms for what we should achieve may not agree with our own beliefs of what we can do—with our levels of just manageable difficulty; and as a result, we are underloaded or overloaded when we try to meet society's expectations.

Usually societal beliefs about capacities are generalizations about a group or class of humans—old or young, male or female, large or small, and so on. The performance standards are then set for that category. There are times and places in history when judgments about capacities based on categories of people are wrong. When children in American schools were first grouped together in classrooms according to age, each child of a given age was considered to have roughly the same capacities and expected to perform to the same standards as all others. But some could not do so because of undiagnosed physical disabilities in hearing, sight, or brain function, dyslexia being a recent example. There were differences in intelligence as well. The dull child, undiagnosed, was expected to perform at the same level as others. The unrecognized gifted child was held back, required to perform below capacity. The emergence of medical examinations of young children and the invention of standardized ability testing provided society with methods for making objective appraisals of a schoolchild's capacity superior to estimates based only on a child's age.

Even so, as I have noted, the true capacities of a person are often inherently unknowable. This is so for two reasons. First, most capacities are not measurable by some yardstick. On the one hand, there might be a man who, as a trained weightlifter, can occasionally lift 400 pounds, thus establishing an estimate of capacity. If in a given contest he lifts 300 pounds, we can say he has shown a "75-percent performance/capacity ratio" in this instance. But most human capacities, such as social skills or creativity, are not measurable in this way. We cannot say how hard we could work in writing a book, making another person happy, training a dog, building a house, investing in the stock market.

Second, it is hard to know what the true limits of a capacity may be. Even in activities like baseball, swimming, or running, where the measurement of performance is standardized, research shows that whenever we think we have seen a performance that exhausts all reserve capacity and reaches the limits of human performance, the next time around the record falls when someone does even better.

The truth of society's beliefs about capacities is one thing; disagreements with the individual about how much of that capacity should be used are something else. What is the proper performance/capacity ratio for a given situation? There are two kinds of conflict between social norms and individual beliefs. In the first, society says "more" and the individual says "less." Here we find the dropouts and underachievers by society's standards. In the second, individuals want to work harder than what is expected and specified. Here we find the rate busters in the piece-work jobs and the recent immigrants who are scholarship winners in the American school and college systems, who are "overachievers" by American standards (though not in their own cultures).

No society wants to destroy itself by testing everyone's limits. Although there are times when human resources have been exploited—mineworkers, children laboring in the garment industry—a successful and humane society needs a reserve capacity, and social performance norms should provide for using less than full capacity most of the time.

The mismatches between the demands of jobs and the abilities of people occur regularly. Some people who are overqualified for their jobs find a way to move up. But for those who have advanced beyond their qualifications, organizations rarely provide ways to step down. Some lines of work do offer ready solutions. A baseball player can move up through the minor leagues over several years until he gets a tryout in the major leagues. If he can make it, he stays; if not, he is truly out of his league; then he can move back down and play very well in the minor leagues, where the demands are less.

Similarly, carpenters who are improving their skills will raise their sights, undertaking increasingly difficult tasks until they reach a challenge they cannot master. Then, like the ballplayer, they can move down a notch and find a level of performance that is right for their abilities.

Ballplayers and carpenters are fortunate. In other occupations, there may be no provision for the one step down to find the right level of difficulty. Few corporations allow downward moves, so that workers who have reached the limits of their capacity and want to ease back are able to do so. We pay for this rigidity through incompetence in high places and through psychosomatic illness and burnout. It is like the TV game show "Wheel of Fortune": the players must either spin and take their chances or "solve the puzzle"; they cannot stop, keep what they have won, and leave the game whenever they wish.

These rules for how hard we should try—whether our own rules or those of society—are always attached to some specific social role, and will change over time. For example, what is expected of the American child's school performance changes constantly. The 1960s' successful launching of Sputnik, the Russian satellite, was interpreted in the United States as evidence that the Russians were getting ahead of this country in the cold war, and that our children must work harder, study more, and produce more to keep the nation competitive.

The rules also will differ from one role to another. In Olympic sports events, an athlete is expected to give 100 percent, to hold nothing back. This is why there are the narrowest of age ranges around peak performance for a sport such as swimming or marathon running, with each sport varying slightly in the age at which the peak occurs. Where a performance requires 100 percent of capacity, the slightest immaturity in development, on the one side, and physical decline as a result of aging, on the other, show up immediately in a weaker performance because there is no reserve to call upon.

In most of our daily social roles, we are expected to make a certain amount of effort—80 percent? 60 percent?—but not to give everything that we have. It would be provocative if we had a ranking of social roles according to how much is expected of us—for example, wife versus husband, worker versus parent. Which are most demanding, and which easiest? How much work does a person do, really, and how different is it during a day or a week across a variety of roles? If we did survey a national sample of our society, asking about the performance/capacity ratios characteristic of different occupations, what might we find?

I doubt that most people in the United States believe that men and women in this country use a high proportion of their talents. Furthermore, I suspect that most people view the effort required by various occupational roles as diverse (for example, that professors work less hard than business executives). But people reporting on their own activities would probably say they are using most of their capacity, whatever others might think about them. There would be individual differences, of course, with some people feeling that they are just taking it easy. For the most part, though, whatever the actual difficulty or the prestige level of a social role, people will say, "Almost nobody really understands how hard I work."

WHO IS HAPPY?

During the past fifty years, social research has produced some findings that appear to me to support the view that one important source of happiness is working at the right level of challenge, wherever that level may be for each of us. This research, which I will describe in a moment, reports that none of our major social characteristics—such as age, income, gender, or education— explains the differences in happiness that exist among us. If we believe it is the challenge more than the material achievement that brings us happiness, and since all of us can create our challenges no matter what place we occupy in society, it follows that happiness is not the property of any particular group, but instead is a quality we create as individuals.

There are other varieties of happiness, of course. There is happiness we gain from our self-respect when we do something right, in contrast with the guilt or shame we feel when we violate our own or our society's standards. There is the intrinsic satisfaction of achieving a goal itself—having food, health, wealth, love; but, as I will say often, the happiness derived from the achievement itself does not last long. When we win, we rest a moment but then move on; the joy of success is soon gone.

The assertion that we are happy when we keep our lives at a level of just manageable difficulty, working on the challenges of that level, brings us directly into one of the ancient philosophical questions about happiness. It is whether an educated, widely experienced, contemplative, sensitive person can be happier than a person without these qualities. Philosophers speak of the full large jug holding more than the full small jug, even though they are equal in fullness. Samuel Johnson is quoted by his biographer, James Boswell, as saying, "A peasant and a philosopher may be equally satisfied, but not equally happy." The assumption is that peasants concentrate on a few physical pleasures and have no higher goals above simple physical gratification. Presumably, it is the achievement of these higher goals that brings greater happiness.

Consider, though, these instances of modest aspiration. Sarah Orne Jewett, in her story "The White Heron," writes of a Southern country girl, awake all night in anticipation of her mission before dawn the next day: to climb the tallest tree along the ocean to spot the home of the white heron.

> There was the huge tree asleep yet in the paling moonlight, and small and hopeful Sylvia began with utmost bravery to mount to the top of it, with tingling, eager blood coursing the channels of her whole frame. . . .
>
> The tree seemed to lengthen itself out as she went up, and to reach farther and farther upward. . . .
>
> Sylvia's face was like a pale star, if one had seen it from the ground, when the last thorny bough was past, and she stood trembling and tired but wholly triumphant, high in the tree-top. Yes, there was the sea with the dawning sun making a golden dazzle over it.

Then, in Ethiopia, there is a river that flows from the mountains to where it disappears into an evaporating lake in the desert. It is a part of Ethiopia toward the coast, where three rift valleys meet. It is described as desolate, awful, one of the most merciless places on earth. Water is the pre-eminent thought in everyone's mind. The residents live under the rule of a sultan, who has a palace of sorts and bodyguards. The residents kill all intruders along the river; the culture is rife with internal murders and ambushes. They live at the edge of survival; they can be attacked at any time and have a constant fear of being ambushed. They essentially live on camel milk and goat milk and rarely eat meat. The women are beautiful; the men, skinny, hard, and wiry. They do not have the gloomy apprehensions of modern life. They are happy with their challenges in life: making their knives out of old railroad materials; making goat milk butter; playing their one sport, a violent game; and ambushing and killing their enemies. As the philosopher Richard B. Brandt observes, "Happiness is not identical with welfare or well-being; a person can be quite happy in a situation which is harmful to him if he does not know that it is, and perhaps even if he does."

In *The Fame Game*, Rona Jaffe says, "It's no fun to be an unhappy movie star, but it's lots better than being an unhappy hooker." Perhaps. In any case, philosophers might take the argument one step farther; that being an unhappy movie star is better than being a happy hooker. Consider a retarded adolescent boy who is filled with satisfaction; he is sitting in the morning sun in the yard at Jackson Lodge, Wyoming, looking over the river at the Teton mountains, feeding gophers popcorn for hours, trying to get them to come and take it from his hand, occasionally succeeding. Would one say that the great philosopher Socrates, when unhappy, may still be happier than the retarded adolescent feeding gophers? But I expect that, in respect to the idea of large and small bottles, it is sometimes the unhappy philosophers who write these thoughts.

Social scientists have made hundreds of studies on the relationship between self-reports of happiness and social-economic characteristics such as income and education. Bear in mind that these are reports by individuals about their own happiness and satisfaction with their life. Some of the questions most often used in these surveys include:

> "These are the best years of my life" (a five-point scale from "strongly agree" to "strongly disagree").
> "Life could be happier" (same scale).
> "Think about your life as a whole. How satisfied are you?" (Scale here is "very satisfied" to "somewhat" to "not at all.")

What people may mean by happiness or satisfaction we cannot tell. Reporting on happiness is like reporting on pain when a medical doctor asks, "How much does it hurt?" We know that we have different degrees of tolerance for pain, and that when one person says, "It hurts a lot," he or she may be reporting a sensation the next person would describe as hardly any pain at all. We have no objective reading, no "pain meter" to calibrate these two. Still, the surveys cover many individuals, using different subjective meanings and frames of reference, with the result that personal differences in standards and meanings cancel out when we compare large social groupings.

Some critics may object that we cannot rely on people to tell us how happy they are; that self-reports of happiness are not true and perhaps even cannot be true; that we lie about how we really feel, and defend ourselves against conscious recognition of our unhappiness; and, finally, that the truth about how we feel is deep in the unconscious and not accessible to survey techniques. These criticisms may or may not be right; I know of no way to test their truth or falsity. The findings I describe here should be taken at face value. They are based on people's own reports on whether they feel happy.

The results of the many studies lead to the same conclusion: there is little or no relationship between social position and one's feeling of well-being and satisfaction with life. Many people describe themselves as happy even under conditions of personal loss, bad health, and low income. In contrast, there are vast numbers of unhappy winners. People at the top are not happier.

The relation between amount of education and subjective well-being was analyzed in a statistical review of more than five hundred studies of this topic. Education has a small positive relationship, but accounts for only 1 percent to 3 percent of differences in subjective well-being. This research finding has not changed over a span of nearly five decades.

Gender does not have an important effect on happiness or unhappiness, although women may be more likely to express their feelings—both positive and negative. For instance, in a national survey of the Canadian population, women reported slightly more often that they feel "on top of the world," or pleased about having accomplished something, or that things are "going their way." However, they also reported more often that they feel lonely or remote, or depressed or very unhappy, or bored and upset.

The effect of race on happiness gets mixed reports. The best present conclusion is that for blacks and whites at the same income level, blacks report slightly lower happiness than whites. These results are drawn from answers to the question "Have you gotten what you expected or wanted or hoped for in life?"

Seven national surveys over the past fifteen years show tiny relationships between advancing age and subjective well-being in various sectors of life: income, community, health, housing, job, and marriage. At the most, only 5 percent of the differences in happiness between people can be accounted for by age; the other 95 percent is caused by something else. When we see older people declining in capacities and becoming dependent, we conclude they will be unhappy. So powerful is this social psychological process that most of us, both young and old, think old age is much worse than older people actually say it is. For example, although more than 50 percent of people over sixty-five say having enough money is a serious problem for the elderly, only 15 percent of this group actually see it as a problem for themselves. Sixty percent of the old say loneliness is a big problem for the elderly, but only 25 percent describe themselves as lonely. Again, 60 percent of the old say adequate medical care is a problem for the elderly; only 10 percent say it is a problem for themselves.

Income is about as unrelated to happiness as are the other social characteristics. Research findings of the past forty years show a positive but very small correlation. The relationship to income is largest at the low end of the income scale. Aristotle wrote in the fourth century B.C., "Happiness seems to require a modicum of external prosperity." And the songwriters Richard Rodgers and Oscar Hammerstein put it, "Money isn't everything (unless you're very poor)." Taking out, say, the bottom 10 percent—where money matters a great deal to those who do not have enough to live on—the relationship between income and happiness for the rest of the population is not of real importance. Rich people are virtually no happier. Even national surveys of young American children (ages seven to eleven) show that their self-reported happiness is not related to their parents' income levels.

Furthermore, studies show no relation to change in national income from decade to decade or among countries representing different economic levels. Americans' ratings of their personal happiness and well-being remained at the same levels from 1957 through 1976. And they were not much different from what they were in the 1940s, although real income in the United States after taxes and inflation could buy a lot more in 1976.

Physical environment also does not matter to happiness. Those who live in the poorer cities, regions, or countries are not less happy than those who live in favored places of wealth.

Many people suffer from insults to mind and body because of the events of fate and the injustices of the social order in which they live. Some are broken, but most manage their difficulties, fit their goals and aspirations to their resources, do the best they can playing the hand life has dealt to them. These facts demonstrate the power of humans to contend with the miserable conditions of their lives, using what capacities they have, and feeling as good about their achievements as the privileged classes do about theirs.

To sum up, the major social characteristics of age, gender, race, income, and education combined can only explain 10 percent to 15 percent of the variation in happiness. I believe that most of the differences between us are caused by our individual actions, by whether we have found a way to live at the level of just manageable difficulty.

II

Thinking About Losing and Winning

3

Did We Win
or Lose?

In the Broadway play *Glengarry Glen Ross*, which is about winning and losing in the real estate business, these things happen to one of the new agents who is engaged in the office sales contest:

He thinks he has won but has not considered the possibility that two clients have given him a phony check and that he is dealing with "crazies."

He is making a sale but another agent badmouths the property, and the customer overhears and cancels the order.

A theft in the office removes all of his contracts, and he has to start over.

He makes a sale but is told by the office head, "That doesn't count,"—something no one has said before; in fact, no one has told him what counts and what does not.

WHAT'S GOING ON HERE?

All of us have lived through something like this, trying to find out what is going on, what the rules of the game are, whether we are succeeding or failing, whether we have already won or lost. To stay on course, we must monitor our progress. We periodically look for disparities between our plans and reality, and try to make midcourse adjustments.

Few acts go unrated. Almost all performances are evaluated by ourselves or by someone else. Although these appraisals differ in intensity, scope, and accuracy, they take place with some regularity. A few "border checkpoints" exist, which, if passed, give us freedom, for a while, from further external appraisals—such as the first year after entering a graduate or professional school, the "honeymoon period"—until we move on to the next border crossing. Or we could move to a place where we are unknown, and might be free for a while from day-to-day appraisals. But this cannot last. A friend said about a midwestern scientist whose work quality was slipping, that he had come east looking for a place to hide but there are none on the East Coast.

In ordinary interpersonal relationships, even intimate ones, there are standards of achievement, although they may be subjective and lack clear-cut criteria for measuring success. And, even if we find one thing to do that is ours alone, perhaps a unique hobby, we still compare our progress to our own internal standards and conclude that we are succeeding or failing.

The fact is that we want information on our progress. We have some ambivalence, of course; but for most of us, most of the time, our need to know the truth outweighs our wish to protect our self-respect. Good performance in one sector of life may mean more than it does in another, of course. A person severely tested every day at work may want a softer life off the job, with less concern about feedback. Conversely, those with a soft job will find another sector of life in which to test themselves. Over all, we are hungry for information that can help us monitor our achievements.

Getting the information is not, though, as easy as it may seem. A lightweight Olympic boxer who lost his fight "told the two newspaper reporters who were present that the decision surprised him. 'I thought I won the first and second rounds,' he mumbled. 'Maybe he was better in the third—I don't know. I thought I was even with him at least.'" Sometimes the information scarcely exists, because there are no good ways to measure progress or achievement. Sometimes other people know but will not tell us.

It is true that occasionally a sharp, abrupt, vivid experience—the moment of truth—tells us what is going on. It may be when you as a youth are not chosen for any team, or are chosen last, or one captain challenges the other, "*You* have to take him." In a work career, it may be a short, direct communication from your employer—a note from your immediate boss, a formal slip from the organization, a face-to-face meeting with a group—in which you are told that this is as far as you go, and not to expect any more promotions or raises. Sometimes we can see the end while still in the middle of the action, like tennis partners in the second set of a doubles match who suddenly realize that they are winning; or like a man trying to win a woman for his wife and suddenly realizing that he will now succeed.

Sometimes the information comes so gradually that we miss it. Usually, however, there is no single event, but rather an accumulation of diverse little episodes over a period—even several years—that gradually intrude into consciousness and reveal what is happening, for better or worse. At work, a chance remark by a co-worker, a report from a friend about how the higher-ups view you, inferences from job assignments, differential promotion rates, raises, furnishings, office or work space, changes in respect from your co-workers—all of these begin to give you a picture of what is going on.

In her poem "The Long Hill," the American poet Sara Teasdale wrote:

> I must have passed the crest a while ago
>   And now I am going down—
> Strange to have crossed the crest and not to know,
>   But the brambles were always catching the hem of my gown.

All the morning I thought how proud I should be
  To stand there straight as a queen,
Wrapped in the wind and the sun with the world under me—
  But the air was dull, there was little I could have seen.

It was nearly level along the beaten track
  And the brambles caught in my gown—
But it's no use now to think of turning back,
  The rest of the way will be only going down.

An analogy from human biology can throw some light on this process of gradual recognition. Cumulative small changes may occur in our bodies—in the composition of the blood, the strength of the heartbeat, or the liver's capacity to store various chemicals. These changes do not show up in our behavior because body organs make hidden compensations to deal with them. Biologists use the concept of "organ envelope" to describe the limit of an organ's functioning within which it can be stretched. But then the stretching exceeds the limit, and the organ collapses, in what is called the "terminal drop": liver stops working, heart stops beating; and suddenly the underlying pathology is evident.

Similarly, in finding out where we stand, we may not see what is taking place; or we may have information but try to avoid it without being forced to a conclusion about what is really going on. But eventually the evidence becomes compelling. There is a "trigger event." We say, "Aha!" The most recent and vivid event finally registers—but it is the end of a longer period of experience.

UNCERTAIN OUTCOMES

In some activities the evaluations of the quality of performance are valid, reliable, clear, and unambiguous. Sports provide the clearest information about how well a person is performing.

In December in the Los Angeles Dodgers' winter training grounds in Florida, aspiring young ballplayers come for initial tryouts. During a morning, fifty pairs of high school students, all pitchers, throw curves back and forth to each other; they are graded by the sharp-eyed Dodgers' scouts who walk up and down the line, taking notes and deciding the future of these young men. For almost a century, baseball statistics in this country have remained the best-kept set of records about career performance and, possibly, about anything at all. The achievements of ballplayers are appraised daily on multiple dimensions, by universally applied measures, whose meanings are agreed upon by all.

Athletes say, "When you walk onto the field, you are running into reality." Konishiki, a 490-pound, 6'2", twenty-five-year-old sumo wrestler from Hawaii, recently won Japan's top sports prize, the Emperor's Cup. He says, "I like the discipline of sumo. It's clear-cut. You win, you go up. You lose, you go down." One of the top squash players in New York City said to me, "I am on the ladder. What am I, eighth or ninth? I seem to beat the people below me and lose to the people above me." Pete Dawkins, the Army football player who won the Heisman Trophy and is also both Rhodes scholar and Wall Street executive, says, "Football is something special at the academies. It's one of the few ways you can actually tell if you succeeded."

Outside of sports, the truth and clarity of the evaluations we receive differ tremendously. In some cases—entrance examinations for élite universities, making money, selecting the first seven astronauts—the information is clear. Stand-up comedians say they have no place to hide from the audience. Some corporations systematically inform their executives about their personal assets and limitations, and research centers on leadership provide performance appraisals and feedback to institutional clients in the armed services, the corporate world, university administration, and many other fields of enterprise. Videotaped episodes selected from group interaction, accompanied by ratings by one's peers and instructors, leave little room for doubt by the recipient.

But in many other professions, such as college teaching, the standards for what constitutes good and bad work are relatively vague. Here there is no "bottom line" that measures performance. Where truth can be evaded or misinterpreted or often ignored, it may take a long time for people to catch on that they are not going any higher. The dean of a faculty of arts and letters in a major university reports to me his extreme difficulty in getting younger faculty members to accept his face-to-face statement that they have gone as far as they can at that university. They find many ways to distort and disbelieve his statement, so when the formal (and legal) written notice comes to them, it is a surprise and a shock.

In some areas of life, the truth of the feedback is not set once and for all; it may improve or get worse over time. Many American school systems have shifted from letter grades by subject to softer measurements of "effort," of attitudes in the classroom, of social skills, of whether one is living up to one's abilities. Promotion from one grade to another used to depend upon performance; if the student failed, the grade was repeated. Now promotion is based in part on age and the social value of keeping pace with one's age mates.

Still, children prefer to learn where they really stand. A friend's daughter at an early age went to a happy school in California where everyone was barefoot, and everyone passed with a "Satisfactory." After moving and transferring to a school in Massachusetts where comparative grades were given, she said, "It was nice to know you were satisfactory, but it's even nicer to know how satisfactory you are."

Those little niches in life, in work careers or elsewhere where the criteria are vague about what is a good performance, provide hiding places to those who wish protection from evaluation. But they are frustrating to those—most of us, really—who want hard information about their degree of success and cannot find any. Administrative officers in American private foundations provide a case in point.

In the United States, there are some twenty-five thousand private foundations that make grants. Probably twenty of these are familiar names—such as MacArthur, Ford, Rockefeller, Carnegie—and the rest are unknown to most of us. They support projects from astronomy to zoology, from art to Zen. Thousands of decisions are made about what areas to go into, who should receive money to do the work, when it is time to change, how a project should be administered.

Foundation administrators have a common interest: each wonders how he or she is doing. Did the grants they made work out the way they thought they would? Are they doing better than expected? Are they doing better than someone else is doing or might do in their place? Can their job, and indeed their foundation, be justified when there are other uses for the money they control? What actually happened as a result of a grant? Did the project or study succeed? Was this project more successful than another of a similar kind? How does this foundation compare with others? Can one conclude that this foundation is better, more successful, than another?

Executives in foundations have a unique position in American society. First, they are cut off from the natural flow of evaluation feedback that occurs in other institutions. There are no voters to elect them and no stockholders to judge their actions. Second, there is no objective way to evaluate the performance of foundation administrators. There are no performance statistics—no batting average or earned-run average. There is no summation showing profit or loss for the year's activity. Dollar value cannot be used as a measure of performance. If a corporation wanted to buy a foundation, as they might a profit-making company, there would be no way to make the usual appraisal.

Foundations lack natural enemies in our society. As a result, while there are some occasional critics and some intelligent challenges, they receive virtually none of the criticism that occurs in other American institutions, such as universities, hospitals, government, and corporations. Furthermore, foundations do not have any deadly competition from other institutions in American life. Foundations have no competing corporations, no competing technologies, no situation of scarce goods or resources, no competition for membership, no dependence on fund-raising drives. They lack the rough-and-tumble of dangerous competition that produces the sharpest information about where one stands vis-à-vis friends and enemies in the day-to-day course of work.

It is not clear why some activities in life have better performance-appraisal information than others. Where numbers—and thus a scale of measurement—are involved, the quality of appraisal is likely to be enhanced. Still, it is not persuasive that numbers are inherent in the nature of sports, but not in politics

or teaching. Do some jobs, being of more value to society, therefore need more accurate evaluations of performance to make
sure the work is done right: astronauts versus U. S. presidents;
baseball players versus foundation executives?

Perhaps it is not only a question of validity. It may also be an
issue of free space in society, of spots or niches or roles that are
not or cannot be evaluated. They may be of fundamental importance in a liberal society, as the zones of unconstrained innova-
tion and experimentation, a counterforce to an Orwellian society
where decision making is concentrated in an all-powerful Big
Brother.

WHO OWNS THE TRUTH?

All societies have customs about who gets what kinds of knowledge and when in life they get it. The cultural wisdom is passed
out according to age, gender, and occupation. There are distribution mechanisms in the family, the schools, the mass media,
and the marketplace where knowledge is either given freely or is
for sale.

One well-known reason for people keeping their knowledge
secret from others is that it gives them special power and privi-
lege and protection (they can hide their mistakes). There have
always been secret societies—that is, the society may not be
secret, but the knowledge shared by the members is kept secret,
as shamans, medicinemen, priests, and magicians do, and as
occurs in the professions of law, medicine, accounting, and psychoanalysis.

Another reason knowledge is held back from people is that
ignorance reinforces traditional values. Society's members never
learn about the alternatives, the ways different from their own
traditions. Information about sex is withheld from children. I
recall the comedian Herb Shriner saying, "I was born in Ohio,
but I moved to Indiana as soon as I heard about it."

In trying to find out whether we are losing, we come up
against situations in which other people know but will not tell us.
Sometimes we lose but do not know it. There are parties we were

never invited to, love affairs that might have been but never got started, none of which are known to us. There are "short lists" for jobs never gotten by us: we can be evaluated for an open position and could almost win, but in the end be turned down and never know this had happened.

Sometimes we do not know we are losing until the very end. Then comes the abrupt dismissal from the job: cleaning out the office while the person is out to lunch, packing the personal papers in cartons ready to move, placing the furniture out in the hall, leaving the office bare. Or, leaving a dismissal envelope on the desk while the person is away on an errand, or putting the pink slip in the pay envelope at the end of the week (most pink slips come as a surprise).

Why should we be unable to find out along the way whether we are losing? One reason is that those who know keep it a secret as long as possible to keep us working in the belief that we can succeed. Some major law firms bring in many more young lawyers than can ever be promoted to partner, and exploit their intense ambition and dedication between the ages of twenty and forty, to get the most work out of them for the benefit of the firm. This occurs, too, in universities at the assistant professor level and in large corporations at the junior executive level. We may want feedback on how we are doing, but it is withheld—even though the decision has already been made about our promotion.

Sometimes we will not tell others that they are losing, or will lose, because we do not want to hurt them. We do not want to be candid to a fault—something all children have to learn. The social philosopher Sisela Bok writes in her book on lying, "Honesty is only one important aspect of human life. Another is not injuring people, which sometimes requires discretion and silence." As the novelist Edith Wharton has said, "Only the fact that we are unaware how well our nearest know us enables us to live with them."

The evasive way we often send bad news makes the information mushy, hard to figure out, and not much help in deciding what to do next. The gentle art of diplomatic rejection is parodied in "Japanese Rejection Slip":

We have read your work with inexpressible pleasure. We swear on the sacred memory of our ancestors that we have never before encountered such a masterpiece. If we publish your admirable work His Majesty the Emperor will undoubtedly insist on its being a model for all future writing and will forbid our publishing any work inferior to yours. Since talents like yours emerge only once in every thousand years, this would put us out of business, and we must therefore refuse your divine work . . . trembling at the thought of the severe judgement we shall receive from future generations for failing to include in our pages, work of such sheer genius.

"Kill the messenger" is our reaction to the bearers of bad news; none of us wants to tell people that they are losers—and then lose our own heads. Studies of school administrators show that school principals and teachers do not want to feel the anger from parents and community by reporting the less able children's poor school performance. They are content to pass the children through the school system without having to tell anyone the truth. Later the children and families become angry at the school when, after graduation, the former students find out in the larger world that they are incompetent.

Our reluctance is even greater when the feedback is to go to a person with power over us. Research on organizational management shows that powerful people get less feedback than others. Success obscures the truth. The honest criticism we may get from equals is degraded into false testimony by differences in social status that develop as the years go by. Nobel Laureates say that after they have won the prize they no longer have access to candid evaluation. It is all very well to say, "Prize your critics," but where is one to find them?

In the executive work career, promotion moves us from the first little apartment in the city to suburban commuting territory and the commuter train. Further success leads to a seat in the private car for hard-working young vice presidents who don't really argue any more the way they used to on the 7:34 local. Young secretaries who used to debate the form of our letters and otherwise keep us sharp are replaced by older executive secretaries who keep their peace and no longer challenge ideas or grammar. Eventually we may rise to a state of complete isolation from feedback and commute to work in the solitude of our own limousine.

When we suspect we are losing and are certain that others know but will not tell us, we fight for the truth. The sick patient in the hospital thinks the doctor, the nurse, and the family are withholding something: "Will I get better or worse, live or die? They will not tell me if I am dying. If forced to tell, they will lie." The patient must move outside the usual feedback channels to get the facts, and asks the hospital orderly or the janitor what they know about the case, trying to find someone who will tell the truth about what is going on.

One might think that it would be easier to find out whether we are winning than whether we are losing; others should be happy to tell us the former. Yet there are times when we are not told we are winning. One of these is when our competitors will not let us know we have the edge. In competition for a contract or a spouse, we do not tell others that we think they are ahead and likely to win, thereby increasing their motivation and weakening our position. Keeping the competition ignorant is to our advantage. We say in a fight, "Don't let the other fighter see he's hurt you," and, in contract negotiations, "Never let them see you sweat."

Nor would we ask our competitors for feedback about ourselves, surprising them with our own naïveté and apparent weakness, and thus deliver ourselves into their hands. Someone else has to tell us we are winning: a mentor or a coach, another member of the team, a friend who stands outside the event.

Often people do not tell us we are winning because they falsely assume that we know we are winning and do not need any feedback. Many people, after telling extremely successful individuals how highly they think of them and their accomplishments, have been surprised by the humble gratitude that follows this confirmation.

Often we are standing on the line between success and failure and do not know it. In competing for a job, a promotion, a business deal, a wife or a husband, or a victory in sports, we may be almost winning but cannot see it. The prospector may be standing on top of a potential gold mine and not know it. Later, if we fail, we will find out how close we came to succeeding, and realize that almost up to the last minute we could have done so, that we barely lost what we could have won.

Such losing may hurt the most. "The tragedy of life is not that man loses, but that he almost wins," writes the columnist Heywood Broun. And the familiar line from John Greenleaf Whittier's poem "Maud Muller" can bring back bitter memories: "For of all sad words of tongue or pen, the saddest are these: It might have been!" We can win or lose by a lot or by a little. After some events when we have lost, we say, "It was no contest," "I was out by a mile," "It wasn't in the cards," "It was never meant to be." But other events are best described as losing by an inch.

For these we cannot escape our belief that had we known, we could have won with just a bit more effort on our part. The close-call events bring many "if's." We see many things that, handled differently, would have produced the win instead of the loss: losing by one plan, failed deadline, phone call, letter, visit, sentence, or word; or by one putt, shot, serve, pass, basket, or pitch.

Without clear feedback, we can be wrong in our judgment of what we are accomplishing. One man with a successful career, a solid happy family, and good health gave up his work to do something else; his wife said to me, "He was winning the race with life and didn't know it." And, among lottery winners of more than a million dollars, at least a dozen never claimed their fortune within the time limit. Perhaps the winning ticket was lost; perhaps the puppy chewed it up; perhaps some of them never knew they were winners.

4

Planning the
Next Actions

Once I see that I have won or lost, I try to analyze what happened and to plan what to do about it. I want to know: "Was I too optimistic about the outcome?" "Did what I did make any difference, or was it just luck?" "Do I get another chance, or is it gone forever?" I work to get more information, think up new lines of action, evaluate the probability of success, and try things out, learn, and revise my plans accordingly.

Most of us value the use of reason, meanwhile recognizing the forces against it. A contradictory philosophical tradition stresses spontaneity, trusting unique impulses, expressing oneself, the supremacy of art over science, and the rejection of deliberate rational action as contrived, artificial, and, in the last analysis, impossible.

In addition, all of us have a bag of mental tricks that we use to deal with both positive and negative achievement gaps even if they do not actually resolve the discrepancies. We evade reality by daydreaming or by magical or wishful thinking. Usually these are responses to loss, and on occasion we use these tricks of redefining reality to achieve a false solace and to maintain our sense of self-worth. When the going gets really tough, we may need to use the more extreme modes of the classic "defense mechanisms"—as psychiatrists call them—such as repression and denial. Each of us harbors powerful wishes that we unconsciously deny, as well as unhappy memories that we have dealt with by obscuring them.

The important point for the purpose of this book is that most of our personality remains open to our conscious awareness and understanding, and our plans express this self-knowledge.

Human beings are not fools, but we are not thinking machines either. Many things go wrong in our decision making. Several are of special significance in understanding how we manage success and failure. First, we may fail to be realistic about the likelihood of winning or losing. Second, we may attribute our winning or losing to the wrong cause. Third, we may be mistaken about whether we will have another chance after losing.

NATURAL OPTIMISM

A fundamental departure from rational action occurs when we decide the probable success of the different actions we might take. Research shows that most of us are overconfident, that we overestimate the likelihood that things will turn out all right, and underestimate risks to ourselves. In general, the more we want something, the more we distort the truth in our belief that we will be successful.

Humans are natural optimists, like Magnum P.I., on the television series, waking up in Honolulu ready to "take another shot at the perfect day." Research in the United States has shown that most people think they will have better-than-average health, live longer-than-average lives, and have better marriages than most. One survey confronted people with a list of 50 negative events, 50 positive events, and 50 that were neutral, and then asked "What is possible for you" in the future? Among events viewed as possible, the positives outnumbered the negatives by almost 4 to 1. Winning does not surprise us, either. We expect to win when we set out.

Our natural optimism helped us to survive over thousands of years because it gave the human race the courage to stand up to the challenges it faced in its evolution. The anthropologist Lionel Tiger speculates that "our benign sense of the future could have been bred into us and other complex animals out of the need to survive." Natural chemicals in the brain and body may "anesthetize the organism against responding too directly and forcefully to negative cognitive stimuli in the environment. They permit the animal to obscure the understanding that its situation is dire." Tiger believes that human beings push ever onward, inextinguishably optimistic in the face of adversity, because of human biology. Optimism and the drive for growth and mastery are part of the same package in our nature.

There are pessimists among us, of course—those who strongly agree with the personality test item "I very often dread the coming day." (Charlie Brown's new philosophy, as he described himself as becoming more optimistic, was, I believe, "Now I only dread one day at a time.") Pessimists can say either that good events will not happen, or that bad events will. It turns out that they favor one or the other style. (Optimism, too, comes in two forms: good events will occur, or bad events will not.)

The pessimists are actually the realists in life. Research on children, for instance, shows that their ratings of themselves on popularity, physical attractiveness, skills in sports, and social behavior will usually err on the positive side, overstating the true case as judged by ratings of them by their teachers and their peers. But about 10 percent of the children show a close correspondence between their self-ratings and others' ratings of them; it is these realistic children who are depressed.

Studies of clinical depression in adulthood show the same pattern: the depressives are more realistic than the nondepressives in their estimates of success, while the overestimators—the optimists—are happier and much more numerous. Other studies have shown that thinking positively or optimistically, even if success is overestimated, can be beneficial to one's health. So, even though wrong expectations may generate more losses than wins in one's life, there appears to be a tradeoff in feeling good.

BELIEVING IN LUCK

In addition to the normal tendency toward optimism, another bias in our thinking appears in the way we assess the reasons for our success. We often view our successes as the result of our own effort and abilities, while we blame our failures on someone or something else, such as bad luck or destiny. When we are winning, we believe: "When I get right down to it, being a success in life is really up to me alone," and, "The most important things that happen to me are usually the result of my own efforts." When we are losing, we say, "The success I'm going to have was already in the cards when I was born, so I might as well accept it and not fight against it," and, "My existence is completely under the control of destiny." It is not often that we hear someone say, "I won, but not because of anything that I did," or, "I lost, and it is all my fault."

In resolving the mismatch between what we want and what we get, we often maintain our self-respect by blaming something or somebody other than ourselves. We say, "Kill the umpire"; we blame the judge; the fighter says, "I was robbed." In response to our child's first social exclusion, failure to make the team, or poor grades, we blame our spouse's family genes for our child's looks, size, and brains. We blame our parents for our weak character, short lifespan, ugly face, fat body, lack of judgment, or inferior education.

Coaches and managers blame their teams instead of themselves. Midwestern bankrupt farmers blame New York City bankers, thus demonstrating that attributions of this kind can become scapegoating on a large scale: the social channeling of anger and aggression from one's own failures into external blame on some socially approved target, often a minority group in our society. We blame our gods; we blame the devil; we blame nature; we blame fate.

If we cannot find somewhere outside ourselves to put the blame, we manufacture something that will serve this purpose. In one of the most striking of the convolutions of human personality, we turn to what psychologists call "self-handicapping." A college student who is unprepared for an exam, and is nearly certain of failure, stays up all night studying and then falls asleep during the exam. Workers who are failing in their job begin to drink during the day so their performance slips even further. Both have created an escape from blaming themselves.

We claim victory for ourselves. When we win in games of chance, we believe we influence the cards, the dice, or the pick of the lottery numbers. In a team effort, when we win we enlarge upon our role and say we played very well; when we lose we blame another player. But when other people win and get ahead of us, we do not explain their success as a result of effort and initiative. Rather, we deride their achievement by attributing it to external factors such as good luck.

The way in which we use the idea of "luck" in explaining winning or losing deserves more analysis. A good starting place is the fact that games in all cultures of the world range from those of pure chance, through those that are a mix of chance and skill, to hypothetical games where the outcome is completely predictable (of course, we do not call the latter "games"). Most cultures have pure chance games similar to craps and roulette. Games of cards usually are a mix of pure chance—the cards dealt to us—and of skill in the way we play them. Chess is mainly a game of skill. The initial layout of the chessboard is always the same. What is unpredictable is the final outcome of a long sequence of moves by us and by our opponent.

Our successes and failures in life may be the result of pure chance. They may have causes we do not understand, cannot control, and often do not even know about. At the other extreme, events may be completely predictable, caused by our own actions, the actions of others, or nonhuman natural forces. Most life events, though, are the result of both known and unknown causes, both controllable and uncontrollable forces.

We make the distinction between games of skill and games of chance, and understand that most are in fact a mix of skill and chance. So it is with winning and losing, a mix of ability and effort with luck. We may go into an event knowing that the outcome is completely dependent on our own efforts—or completely dependent on chance. Most often we see it as a mix of these two. Proverbs tell us that chance favors the prepared mind; that luck is the residue of design. We make our best effort and say the rest is up to fate.

We describe some people as "lucky"—favored by chance, successful through causes other than their own actions or merit—in reference to a specific event, to being in the right place at the right time. An example is the person who wins a lottery, in which the odds of winning are 1 in 10,000,000. We also speak of "bad luck," "being down on our luck," "out of luck," a "stroke of luck," "to try our luck." We say, "His luck has turned at last," "Better luck next time," "His luck is running thin," "His luck ran out." A New York City tourist epitomizes the bad luck example: while sightseeing in New York City, strolling with his family along an avenue, this man was killed by a five-pound dumbbell that rolled off the windowsill of a high-rise apartment where another man was doing morning exercises.

Are there lucky and unlucky people? We say certain people are lucky when they win by chance more often than would be expected. And, statistically, there are such people. Imagine 1,000 people each of whom has had 20 winning or losing events in life to be determined by chance. Now imagine fate flipping a penny 20 times for each of these 1,000 persons, where heads means a favorable outcome and tails means a loss. We know that most people would have a mix of heads and tails. But a few people at the extremes of the chance distribution would inevitably have many more of one than the other. One or two people might get all heads or all tails—lucky and unlucky persons.

Events that have a large element of chance fall into two classes: involuntary and voluntary. The first category includes some exotic cases of drawing lots, cutting cards, or rolling dice to see who must go on a dangerous scouting mission or who goes overboard on the overcrowded lifeboat so that the ship's other passengers may live.

The second category, voluntary participation, such as buying a lottery ticket, seems puzzling. Why would people do this unless they thought they were lucky, or perhaps secretly believed they could influence the outcome? Research on lottery behavior reveals that people think they have a better chance of winning when they select their own numbers for the lottery than when they are given random ones. Choice gives people the illusion of control. Even when we perceive the true situation, we turn to lucky charms, to magic, to prayer in the belief that we can control our chances. One month the New York State lottery prize was $30 million. Millions of people bought tickets. An observer of the three days before and the three days after the drawing of the winning number noted that even though everyone knew the outcome was pure chance, nevertheless many said things like, "I've got this wired," and really believed that they would win. Not many were revealing their inner hopes or fantasies or magical methods of control.

What happens afterward? Bereft of our fantasies of winning, daily life becomes very plain for a while. Imagining winning, even when we know the odds are one in millions and the result not under our control, still leaves a residue of failure when we lose. Fortunately, since we know that the result was pure chance, we do not blame ourselves—or mutter "I should have chosen those other numbers I was considering"—or do we? And we do not blame outside forces. We would not blame God for losing the lottery—or would we?

In thinking about the causes of achievement gaps, we may believe something is a chance event when in fact it is predictable, perhaps even under our own control. Or, the reverse, we may believe that an outcome is predictable, even controllable, when in fact it is mostly chance. These are honest errors involving ignorance, or a misreading, of the nature of the causes involved.

These errors are very different from the distortions that arise from attempts to protect oneself, to enhance self-esteem, to blame others for one's own mistakes. When we distort, we may blame chance when in fact we really know that our own actions were the main cause of losing. We claim credit for wins that are clearly the result of chance—even believing that we controlled the roll of the dice or influenced the decision of the gods.

These two modes of dealing with life—wearing rose-colored glasses and blaming someone or something else for what went wrong—seem so useful in keeping up our self-respect, or sense of well-being, that one has to ask, "Why doesn't everybody do this all the time?"

Two obvious, powerful forces set limits to what we can get away with, keeping us from excesses of self-deception. We might think of the first of these as the impact of reality, and the second as the restrictive influence of social rules. Both a more or less correct estimate of the probability of success and a correct assignment of cause to oneself or to external forces are necessary to survive hunger and injury. A person can be successful in holding off reality as the gap between aspiration and achievement widens—until a crash occurs. A successful man who wanted to be even more of a celebrity in the city blamed his inability to make it on the career sacrifices he believed he had made on behalf of his wife. He drove his wife away by blaming her for his failures, and she left him for another man in spite of all he thought he had done for her. Once he had driven her away, there was no one left for him to blame, and he committed suicide.

The social rules that define what is acceptable self-deception probably had their origins in a pair or a team or a tribe's deciding whether a win or a loss was its own fault, and whether they were wrong in their expectations. "I thought it was a close contest." "No, we weren't in it." "I was sure we were going to win." "Yes, and we should have beat them." Or, "No, the stars were in the wrong position." Social pressures will push toward reality. A *New Yorker* cartoon portrays a woman speaking forcefully to her husband: "It is *not* in the lap of the gods! It's in *your* lap, dammit!" At other times, we are told we are too hard on ourselves, taking too much blame for some consequence when we were really not responsible for what happened. Over time, cultural ideologies evolve to account for individual and group failure and success.

What is agreed upon will vary between different historical epochs and societies. Greek mythology had a tragic view that saw humans as creatures limited by forces beyond their control. Humans had power and ability but were subjected to the unpredictable interventions of the gods. Today a professor at Wesleyan University, Phyllis Rose, describes how the students there are unable to accept that the gods intrude, take sides, play tricks, that "Zeus keeps two jars by his doorway—one filled with good, one with evil. He throws both down indiscriminately." They believe instead that good prevails and the bad die young, and there is no such thing as bad luck: illness, evil, and death are punishments for character flaws.

In the end we lose or win more than we expected because of errors in our theories about the world and ourselves. We calculate costs, probabilities, and resources, choosing actions we believe will bring success. The outcomes are always partially caused by forces we cannot predict and often do not even know about. Mistakes in judgment come from our unconscious desires, incurable optimism, false attribution of cause. We have large zones of uncertainty, and the results of our actions often fall far from the mark. As in football, though we get hit behind the line now and then, we also run for unexpected touchdowns.

SECOND CHANCES

In dealing with loss, we make a distinction between events that come around again and those that happen only once. I may have a second, or a third, or unlimited chances to try and succeed. Or, I can win back what I lost; I think, "What was lost could be mine again." Some events come only once in a life and present the only chance I will ever have: I win or I lose, and it is over. A hypothetical distribution of life events by a number of chances might show that most opportunities repeat themselves—two, three, four, five times, with perhaps some whose recurrence is unlimited; and that once-in-a-lifetime events are few. My reasoning will depend on our definition of the event. If it is over and gone forever, I must give up my goal. If I believe I still have a second, or a third, chance to succeed, I start making my plans.

We like to know we will have another chance, even when the probability of winning is reduced. In the field of research in psychology called "risk preference," people are asked to try to draw a red marble out of a jar they cannot see into. In one case, the red marble is mixed with nine white marbles, and one can draw only one time. In another case, ten red marbles are mixed with ninety white marbles, and one can draw ten times. Although the probability of taking out the red marble by chance is the same in both cases (1 in 10), people prefer to have the ten chances.

Some psychologists say people behave this way because they do not understand that the odds of winning are the same. Perhaps this is true of some of us, but I think it is mostly the human preference for more than one chance combined with our innate optimism. We believe that we can do better the next time. Where it is a matter of skill and we have learned something, that belief is probably justified. But even when we know it is a matter of pure chance, we want to try again in the belief that our luck will change for the better.

Despite our desire for another chance, we sometimes face opportunities that are truly "once in a lifetime" events, such as the Olympics. An advertisement in *Sports Illustrated* has a picture of a woman sprinter in the Olympics 100-meter dash and the caption "How does it feel when you train ten long years for ten short seconds?" Adidas, the shoe manufacturer, goes one better in its ad showing a sprinter at the starting blocks under the caption: "He has waited a lifetime for the next ten seconds." Whether they win or lose, contestants such as these will probably be too old to compete in the next Olympics four years hence.

Sometimes the one-time events come from the way our society is organized. In chapter 8, I describe how work careers can be divided into those that are programmed and those that are episodic and segmented. A most popular description of episodic achievement is in the lyrics of the song "There's No Business Like Show Business." An actor or an actress who fails to get a part in a play, a film, or a television show may soon have another chance for a different part that is just as good. The play, the film, the TV show, is good or bad, succeeds or fails. No matter; if it fails, the next one can succeed. These are episodic careers with second, and more, chances.

In a programmed career, in contrast, there are once-in-a-lifetime opportunities for which being in the right place at the right time is essential. The chance for advancement comes but once. If a man or a woman is passed over, or unknown, it is gone. Kenneth Prewitt, senior vice president of the Rockefeller Foundation, describes the three-part career trajectory that works for the top 5 percent in universities, business, the law, and other élite occupations. Part 1: Get through the educational system with a successful record and into the job market at a suitable entry level. Here the important factor in success is social background or social class origin and its influence on education. Part 2: Work hard so that you move steadily upward to higher levels until you reach a "platform" (actually better described as a "launching area")—usually around the age of forty to forty-five. The important factors that affect winning or losing here are motivation and hard work; the outcome is closely related to performance.

Part 3: Be lucky enough to be selected for a major advance into one of the top positions in society, as a university president, the CEO of a major corporation, the head of a major law firm. At this point, there are more talented candidates than there are top positions; inevitably, there is competition for limited vacancies. The talents of the candidates are about equal, and the most important influence on the outcome is luck—being in the right place at the right time at the right age. These top jobs in the key institutions in our society open up about every fifteen years, on the average; and if the position is filled with somebody else, the opportunity is gone forever.

One-time events also are created simply by making social rules. In England, for instance, in previous centuries, debtors were put in prison. Today the laws on bankruptcy give us a second chance to become financially sound. The creditors, usually a bank, advise us that the way to manage is to consolidate the small debts, stretch out the time period for payment, lower our level of living, and gradually pay off.

Young criminals once were sent directly to prison. Now juvenile offenders arrested for the first time will get off free, sometimes even a second and third time. A law school graduate is allowed, in New York State, three tries to pass the bar examination to be admitted to the practice of law. A graduate student in psychology can take a second shot at passing the Ph.D. oral exam. In politics one can try and try again to be elected to a particular office. At some point, though, the social norms are expressed in ridicule—"Doesn't know when to quit"—as when Harold Stassen, who began trying in 1948, made his ninth try to get the

Republican nomination for President of the United States.

We can try to change the rules that keep us from having another chance—change the system, start the revolution. We can use a substitute mode of dealing with the achievement gap by turning to fantasy of how we might have done it differently. We read novels: *Seconds,* or *Replay.* We go to the movies. In the 1988 film *Peggy Sue Got Married,* a woman travels back in time and changes her life story. She is nice to her little sister, her parents, her grandparents, to the class nerd; she does have the affair with the poet; she tells off her high school enemies; she improves the first years of her marriage.

Sometimes the social rules encourage us to try again even if we do not want the second chance. We tell our children to keep trying until they win. We send soldiers back into battle for a third or fourth offensive. We will set our own internal standards—guided perhaps by the image of Humphrey Bogart slipping over the side of the *African Queen* one more time into the shallow, leech-infested river to try again to find a way into Lake Victoria.

The rules on second chances change over time. During the middle part of the twentieth century, it was customary in the American public school system to have students' records passed on from one grade to the next so as to create a cumulative file. The kindergarten teacher's ratings of one's behavior and personality were still in the file in tenth grade. These student files were private: that is, neither parent nor student was permitted to examine the dossier and to correct errors or challenge the appraisal. No recognition was given to the likelihood that a child would change from age five to fifteen. Instead, a child was marked early and secretly. A stigma often was placed on a young child—"has tantrums," "wets pants," "is moody, restless," "does not get along well with other children," "seems poorly motivated for schoolwork." In the fall, teachers reading through the files of their assigned students formed impressions of the children based on the uncorrected record.

Beginning about 1970, as it became understood that children change from year to year, many schools took action to destroy the earlier records. A member of a suburban school board recalls the day when she loaded her station wagon with all of the student records in the school that were more than three years old and drove them to the town dump for incineration. The students were permitted a fresh start, a second chance.

As I have noted, our plans depend in part on whether we anticipate having a second chance to reach our goal. Sometimes we will be wrong. The unfaithful husband who wants desperately to restore his ruined marriage but believes it is all over, is unprepared when his wife says, "I've decided to give you another chance."

We may believe we do have a second chance, even a third, fourth, or fifth, when in fact there are many more. We stop trying when we could continue. Five of the best-selling books of this century were first rejected by more than a dozen publishers: Dr. Seuss's *And To Think That I Saw It on Mulberry Street* (rejected by twenty-three publishers); Richard Hooker's *M*A*S*H* (rejected twenty-one times); *Kon-Tiki*, by Thor Heyerdahl (twenty rejections); *Jonathan Livingston Seagull* by Richard Bach (eighteen rejections); and Patrick Dennis's *Auntie Mame* (rejected by seventeen publishers).

Or, we may think we will have another chance and only later realize we will not. On his way to an appointment, a man might be walking by a store in San Francisco and see in its window a tie that seems perfect—just the tie he has been looking for for a long time. He tells himself that he will come back tomorrow and buy it. But when he returns the next day, the tie is gone and the salesman says that it was the last; there will be no more because the bolt of material was printed only once. Everyday errors of judgment like this—making us miss our one chance—may lie behind the saying that in the end we are more sorry for what we did not do than for what we did do.

5

Can We Make
the Change?

"**C**an the leopard change his spots?" asks the prophet Jeremiah. We say also, "You can't teach an old dog new tricks." But we also have what might appear to be a national fantasy that we can become whatever we want to be. From simple New Year's resolutions to undergoing transsexual operations, most of us are trying to become something that we are not but hope to be. The multitalented performer Steve Allen has written, somewhere, "Most of the people you talk to in the course of a day used to be someone else"; and a model on a TV interview show, when asked, "Did you look like this when you started?" says, "I didn't look like this yesterday." What is happening is that we are living during a revolution in ideas and behavior that began in the 1960s and has picked up speed in the past two decades.

THE NEW CULTURE OF CHANGE

The main theories about human development used to say that early childhood has a lasting effect on our personalities as adults.

The psychologists argued that it is difficult to get rid of behavior we learned in our early years because it became part of us before we were old enough to understand consciously how and why we learned it. Psychiatrists and psychoanalysts believed that we never resolve intense childhood conflicts but only find new ways to deal with them; essentially, only our defenses change. Sociologists told us that the ways we classify and label our children—dumb, smart, ugly, beautiful—produce self-images in them that may last through life. Pediatricians and other physicians believed that because nutrition affects physical growth, poor nutrition in childhood may permanently affect how well the brain works in adult life.

New facts and theories about human development are in sharp contrast to some of these older ideas. In this new view of development, although our early years are influential, we have a capacity for change throughout our entire life. The course of our development is much more open than used to be believed. The burden of proof in science is now on those who assert that early experiences are strongly linked to personality and behavior in later life.

The sciences of human behavior that used to focus on the limits and constraints on human development are now the sources of liberation and enhancement of human development. We have learned that nearly every molecule in our bodies is replaced many times through the lifespan, except for neuronal DNA and collagen. The ways of creating change in our bodies and behavior are increasing. The metamorphosis of body and mind is possible through new scientific technologies. In addition to organ transplants, plastic surgery, and genetic surgery, there are behavior therapy, behavior modification, and drug therapy for depression and other mental ills. We can change a person's bones, heart, face, and sex; and these heroics of a decade or so ago are now a common experience.

These profound changes in our understanding of human development should lead us from the one-shot vaccination model of improving development to a continuing investment in human betterment through the lifespan. Changing diets in later life may reduce and often reverse the effects of early malnutrition as brain chemistry can be altered; training programs in problem solving and memory during our adult years improve these capacities and sometimes may be even more effective than teaching during childhood periods. Preschool education programs for disadvantaged children should be followed by continuing special educational programs through the later years so the early gains do not fade away.

One outcome all of us can applaud is the liberation of mothers from the undeserved guilt they carried when everything that turned out bad in a child was blamed on their infant care practices. Too much emphasis was placed on the effects of parental behavior during a child's first few years of life, and parents unnecessarily have had to carry the heavy burden of the cultural belief that the child is fragile and that what happens in adulthood is the parent's fault. Children are stronger and more resilient than most parents believe; and injuries, whether physical or emotional, in the early years of life are often remedied by the experiences of later years.

At the same time that these revolutions in the biomedical and psychological sciences are taking place, social rules and customs are being altered. Many millions of people are trying to change themselves day by day, trying to be better, trying to be something more than they are now. Although self-improvement is not new in human history, and certainly not in the United States (where we have had the Chautauqua lectures, Dale Carnegie courses, and the Moral Rearmament movement), what is new is that social norms now are more permissive about such changes. These more relaxed norms permit us to leave a confining group and find one that is more supportive.

Each age and place has its own theories of human nature in the form of myth, legend, and religious belief. Such theories deal with the goodness or evil of humankind, with what is inherited and what is learned, and with whether humans are dominant over, subjected to, or simply part of nature. The possibilities of human metamorphosis are present in three great classes of stories about human transformation: creation myths; legends about transformation upon death and existence after death; and myths about lifespan development.

The primary source of these tales in Western civilization is our popular literature, ranging from the great myths and legends of the past to their counterparts in television, film, magazines, newspapers, and fiction and nonfiction of the present time. Our treasured stories about metamorphosis in children—*Alice in Wonderland, Pinocchio, Snow White, Peter Pan*—are especially poignant because they engage children's fascination with transformation of self. A representative group of well-known tales might begin with the pre-Egyptian legends of Osiris, continue through Ovid's *Metamorphoses* and the story of Paul's conversion to Christianity on the road to Damascus, and end with the travel writer Jan Morris's account of her early years as a boy and man and ultimate recognition of her true "shape" as a woman.

During the past five thousand years, there has been a change in our ideas about and attitudes toward human metamorphosis: from the belief that such transformations required supernatural causes or natural, external forces to the belief that we can do it ourselves; from punishment by society for attempting such transformation to the vast support system we now have for people who want to change.

Folk literature illustrates how our view of transformations has itself been transformed. The famous legend of Dr. Faustus, a learned German doctor who in the sixteenth century sold his soul to the devil in exchange for youth, knowledge, and magical power, is the subject of several great works of literature. In Christopher Marlowe's *Dr. Faustus* (1593), he comes to a bad end. In the several versions of Johann Wolfgang von Goethe's *Faust* (1808–33), he comes to either a neutral or a good end. The Choir of Angels speaks the motto, "He who exerts himself in constant striving, Him we can save." Gradually, by the end of the nineteenth century, the belief in the possibility of changing oneself became acceptable. Today many men and women in midlife believe that personality change is possible for them through their own efforts.

The historical evolution of our beliefs and attitudes about human transformation and the capacity to change parallels a general increase in our knowledge of human nature and in our concern with each person's rights and dignity. In Western culture, the idea of the possibility of human transformation is a liberating force that joins the ideas of humanitarianism, democracy, and freedom.

In keeping with the beliefs and values of our society, most of us do change over the lifespan, even if gradually. Personality change is not like a science fiction jump through hyperspace to another, different world; nor is it like switching the radio to another program. At any particular time, a person may be changing in some of his or her personal characteristics, while most of the others remain much the same. Still, over the years, a significant number of characteristics will not be the same. The person now is different—although in any given year one seemed distinctly stable.

People differ in how they feel about changing. Some agree with these personality test items: "Sometimes I feel I'm changing very fast"; "I've noticed that my ideas about myself seem to change very quickly"; and "Most people must think of me as a very changeable person." Others agree with these: "If I could be what I would most like to be, it wouldn't be very different from what I am now"; "I'm pretty much the same no matter whom I'm with"; "I expect to be about the same a year or two from now"; and "I can't imagine myself as different from the way I am."

And, within ourselves, we still have mixed feelings about trying to change. Almost no one would give up who he or she is— one's own identity—to become someone else, even if the life were to be vastly better. Although we want to change, we also need to maintain our sense of identity and continuity of self, to avoid changing too fast or being forced to change against our will by outside forces. The heroic efforts of political prisoners and prisoners of war to maintain their identity under the stress of isolation and torture are as much a part of the nobility of human character as are the companion heroic efforts of humans to become something more than they are now.

REWRITING OUR LIFE HISTORIES

All of us have images and memories of the selves that we have left behind as we move on through life. And we have images of undesirable selves we have chosen not to be. We take pride today when we see someone else who took the path we wisely avoided. We have images of ourselves in the past that we do not like—of a person we once were but have overcome and are no longer. Some of us are haunted by images of ourselves that we have lost or abandoned. We may feel some guilt about these, like the upwardly mobile immigrant who has moved far from ethnic roots and values. We may feel sadness: a survey of several hundred midlife corporate executives found that more than half had wanted to become professional athletes, still believed that they could have made the grade, and viewed that lost option as a lost self. I think of Marlon Brando in the taxicab scene in *On the Waterfront* (1954), with his heart broken, saying, "I could have been a contender. I could have been somebody. Instead of a bum—which is what I am."

Our images may be of good or bad or lost or abandoned selves, but there is one overriding characteristic: they can be changed. Sometimes we tinker with the evidence. Aldous Huxley, in his foreword to a paperback edition of *Brave New World* published some thirty years after the first edition, comments on the futility of trying to improve or patch up imperfections in one's earlier performance—"To spend one's middle age trying to mend the artistic sins committed . . . by that different person who was oneself in youth . . . is surely vain and futile"—and refers to himself as "an older, other person." Nevertheless, some artists buy up their earlier paintings to destroy them, and some authors seek to obtain—and destroy—letters they wrote in earlier years.

Usually we change only our memories of what we were like. The *New Yorker* writer Brendan Gill states two main reasons for changing our subjective life histories: to maintain a sense of continuity and identity in the midst of personal change, and to increase our self-respect:

One spends a lifetime reconstructing one's past, and it is not merely in order to find an image of oneself that will prove pleasing; rather, it is in order to approach some tentative, usable truth about oneself by ransacking all the data that have hovered dimly somewhere "out there," helping to form one's nature.

Our subjective life history is soft, pliable, and easily changed to make us think better of ourselves. Most of us have thought, "if I had my life to live over again, I'd do things very differently." Although we cannot actually live it over, we can transform it in our minds. We can say that we never wanted—or no longer want—something that we did not get. We can say that we could have reached a goal if we had tried harder, or if someone had not restrained us, or if we had more time, or if we had been endowed with a different, better set of skills. And, after a major success that has taken years to achieve, we can change our reasons for having pursued it so long. This is similar to the kind of rewriting or correcting of personal history that occurs at a deeper level in therapy. Psychoanalysis as well as other therapies can be seen as a way of helping people change their view of their own history, to add into the picture experiences that were repressed, and especially to give a different interpretation and meaning to the memories of what happened.

That we change our memories to increase our self-respect is widely understood. Less well understood is how we alter our memories to create coherent stories of our lives that explain our place in life and account for what happened to us. Both winning and losing are involved and must be fitted into the story. As these events occur and change who we are, the past must be revised to fit the present and the future, creating the appearance of an orderly process of development from beginning to end. We rework our images of who we used to be to make them lock into our images of ourself today and of what we hope to become. In this sense, the present and the future determine the past.

So powerful is this desire for consistency that we may even rewrite the past to make it worse than it was, to fit a present self-image that is low in self-respect. If we fail today in some endeavor, we go back and resketch the past to show the thread of failure—where it started and how it brought us to the current hard time.

Because the reconstruction of the past is often made public—in discussion, autobiographies, personal statements—there is a limit to how far we can distort reality. This limit is set by the memories others have of our past. A man or a woman may be surprised to hear a spouse's new version of an event from their shared past. It might be about how they met, why they were married, what they had hoped for in earlier years, why they have a particular number of children. And so it is with parents and their children's versions of family events from the past, and with companions in the workplace rewriting their memories of shared careers.

Sometimes couples, families, or work companions cooperate to create a new shared image of some past event—a collective rewriting of history. More often, though, husband or wife, or parent, or brother or sister, will challenge the new version, arguing about the right to make this change and about what "really happened," until the subjective life history is driven back underground where the person can think almost anything and remain unchallenged.

In general, in the reconstruction of one's life history in public, there are constraints and social rules about what may be said, or what one can get away with. It must stay near the truth—truth being the shared version of the past event; and a person is checked by others who shared the experience and must agree that this version is within the limits of the truth.

In order to be free to change the past around as they wish without being monitored, many people never reveal their views. Even so, at times they need to escape the censor. A professor told me that many of her male colleagues at a second-level university admitted to her that one factor in their divorce and remarriage was the desire to bury the knowledge of their earlier aspirations (which their first wives knew only too well). Thus, they could convince others that a professorship at this university was the height of their youthful aspirations, when in fact they had viewed it as a steppingstone to Harvard, Yale, or Stanford.

Both biographies and autobiographies are under these social constraints. Biographers stick to the facts perhaps more than people do who write about themselves, but still the facts they use are sometimes selected to tell a story, and often there are gaps in information where the biographer is free to interpret and to create a story line. But their works, too, are reviewed by others knowledgeable about the subject and hence constrained by challenge and correction. The autobiographer may be more free, as at first appeared to be the case in the books written by Richard Nixon and members of his staff and cabinet in the years following Watergate. Still, these books so distorted publicly known facts that the books were widely challenged, and many citizens could only shake their heads and ask, "Do they really believe this is what happened?"

The rewriting of life history is done in pieces and in sections, reflecting the way our sense of self is structured. This fragmentation permits us to tell a story about a particular part of our life to others who are not familiar with it and cannot check the truth. Thus, we can get away with telling a story about a past sports achievement to companions at work. In the book *Shoeless Joe* (1983, by W. P. Kinsella; the basis for the film *Field of Dreams*), an old man who claims he was a former major league baseball player for the Chicago Cubs, says, "If I can't have what I want most in life, then I'll pretend I had it in the past, and talk about it and live it and relive it until it is real and solid and I can hold it to my heart like a precious child."

As is the case with daydreaming, the absence of social controls over our fantasies allows us to get farther and farther from reality. We can change our memories around and get away with it when no one knows our past.

THE MYTH OF LIFE STAGES

The belief that we are able to change ourselves and the course of our lives is countered by the belief that our personalities and life paths are locked into stages of development beyond our control.

The truth is that many stage theories of human development are excessively deterministic about what happens to us in life. Most of life remains unpredictable, full of unexpected twists and turns, although open to our successful intervention at strategic points when we choose to exercise our powers.

Imagine that you could look ahead at life from birth and see the thousands of events you would confront. Some are biological in nature: normal alterations in body size, bone structure, and hormones as you develop, or abnormal changes due to illness and disability—arthritis, cataracts, deafness. Other events are social/economic/political: marriage, starting a family, establishing a home; living through a depression or a revolution. Still others will come from the physical world: earthquake, fire, a loose step or a falling rock on a mountain trail. And there are psychological events: religious conversions, resolutions to devote your life to your family, changing orientations toward time when you start counting years left to live rather than years since birth; moments of suspicion that you have, on balance, done more harm than good to humanity.

Many events in our lives are predictable; we can see them coming. Often they are the result of our own action; we wanted to make them happen, and we did. Even so, it is hard to see far into the future because there are too many contingencies. Tiny uncertainties add up to one big uncertainty about what lies ahead. Moreover, major events that impinge upon our lives come from the outside, unforeseen and unimagined, making it even less possible to foretell the future.

Nonetheless, we try to predict our own life course rather than live in uncertainty and worry. And we attempt to do so by saying that there are predictable stages in our lives related to how old we are. And if we believe in stages of human development, we have an explanation why certain things happen to us; we have words or phrases to hang things on as we go along.

The idea of stages can also provide a person who is in the midst of a change in behavior or personality, with an easily understood explanation of it, and thus avoid the necessity of giving the true reason which others may find strange and hard to accept. Thus, however valid, the notion of stages is a convenient, socially useful theory of human development, which helps bring people together with a shared sense of trust and predictability.

The word *stage* has interesting origins. One of these refers to the vertical portions into which a building is divided, and from this meaning comes the idea of a series of levels rising stepwise one above the other. Another comes from travel and refers to the place in which a rest is taken on a journey, especially a regular stopping place on a stagecoach route. From this comes the idea of a journey through life, with stopping points. Synonyms today include *turning point, transition, phase,* and *passage.*

Social and behavioral scientists have been trying to describe *stages* for at least a century. Economists who study the family use the term *life cycle,* which dates from the establishment of the social security program in England in the early 1900s and refers to the "cradle to grave" cycle of dependency. Sociologists use the term *life course* development and focus on the changes in social roles that people make during their lives. Historians use *life history,* and biographers and novelists refer to *life stories.* Psychologists consider *lifespan development.* All agree that there are many life events that are correlated loosely with chronological age.

Nevertheless, if the idea of life stages is to be useful in forecasting the future, it must pass certain tests. First, how closely tied is the event to a particular period of years? At one extreme we might imagine that everyone confronts a particular event upon reaching a certain age—say, thirty-five. Or, the relationship may be loose, so that 15 percent of people will experience this event at age thirty-five; but for some it occurs at age twenty, and for others at age fifty.

Second, does it happen to most people? Or are only some individuals affected, and unpredictably at that? Do only certain subcultural groups face this event, by reason of where they live or how rich they are?

A third test is whether the stages are supposed to be true through history or are affected by social change. Once we might have said that childbearing and child rearing are stages that follow marriage, but this is not the case for a significant percentage of the United States population today.

Fourth, is the life event part of an invariant sequence in our development that may speed up or slow down, but cannot be altered—as a child must walk before it runs?

Fifth, does the event have the same effect on almost everyone? The fact is that people react differently to historical events. Devastating as, say, the Black Plague, the Napoleonic wars, and the Great Depression may have been for society as a whole, individuals did not suffer these events identically. On the other hand, what would be a minor, inconsequential experience for most of us may change another person's life. The deck is full of all kinds of cards, but even the same card will fit differently and have a different value in every hand.

The current "stage theories" of human development span the three scientific fields of biology, sociology, and psychology. Of the three fields, research on biological stages of development describing changes from conception on through adolescence is the oldest and most fully developed body of work. The characteristics studied may be at the level of behavior, such as walking or talking, or at the level of molecules and cells, studying tissue development and how specific organs such as the brain develop. These biological stage models are on the whole accurate at early ages, but less so in adulthood because people become less uniform biologically as they age.

Sociological stages of the life course reflect the fact that every society assigns its members to positions in society. A series of "status passages"—a sequence of changes from birth to death—punctuates an individual's life. Stages are described as "developmental tasks" that arrive at a certain age period in life.

These sociological ideas are built on the assumption of a stable society, with no change over time. But obviously today's societies are changing rapidly. A sequence of status passages may be broken. Correlations with age may change from one decade to the next. Education, work, and leisure are being more equally distributed across the lifespan, rather than being lumped, respectively, into early, middle, and late age periods of life. (Just one example: eighty-five-year-old Daniel Wynkoop graduated in the Yale class of 1991.) Family patterns over the years are altered by the increased participation of women in the labor force, by the need to care for aging parents, and by the downwardly mobile young adults who survive by coming home to live with their middle-aged parents.

The third group of stage theories comes from psychologists. We should separate those that deal with childhood and those concerned with adulthood and old age. During childhood, a period when there is a particularly strong biological force in development, some characteristics are closely tied to age. Some psychological events, such as the emergence of self-awareness and of a sense of moral rules during the last half of the second year of life, also fit the criteria for a true stage. Similarly, the descriptions of intellectual development in childhood are powerful and valid stage formulations.

Where later age periods are concerned, though, life is not so orderly. While one might say in the popular sense that "everyone goes through stages," the truth is that the events usually attributed to specific stages are not alike for different people and happen at different ages. The noted developmental researcher Bernice L. Neugarten says:

> The psychological themes and preoccupations of adults, although they are often described by psychologists as occurring in succession, do not . . . arise at regular moments in life, each to be resolved and put behind as if it were a bead on a chain. Identity is formed and reformed. Issues of intimacy and autonomy and commitment to significant others, the pressures of time, the reformulation of life goals, stocktaking, the acceptance of successes and failures—preoccupy the young adult as well as the old adult. The themes recur, emerging and re-emerging in new forms over long periods of time. It is therefore a considerable distortion to describe the psychology of adulthood and old age as a series of discrete stages, as if adult life were a staircase.

The psychological stage theories for adult life are based on studies of small numbers of subjects—mostly men—who do not represent the diversity of people in society. They are essentially a group of case studies. We can think of psychological stage theorists as humanists and poets. They have identified some powerful life experiences and, in this way, helped us to think about these events and to share the experiences. But it seems less useful to attempt either to tie these experiences closely to chronological age or to put them into a sequence, when the evidence stands against doing so.

6

How Free Are
We to Act?

We have the ability to change, but are we free to do so? We are surrounded by the beliefs and sentiments of others about what goals we should desire, how high we should aim, how fast we should get there, and which actions we should take. For each of us there are particularly important people or groups whose good opinions and approval we especially want. In considering our changes, we take into account the reactions that such people may have. Our desire for their approval emerges from our natural human fear of being unable to fulfill basic needs such as hunger and warmth. We associate the satisfaction of these needs with the approving and accepting presence of another human, at first almost always our mother. The infant grows to recognize that meeting basic needs is dependent on the favorable judgment of others.

The word *socialization* refers to a process of learning by which we are prepared, with varying degrees of success, to meet the requirements laid down by other members of society for our behavior in a variety of situations. These requirements are attached to one or another of the recognized roles in our society, such as husband or wife, daughter or son, student, employee or boss, or citizen of the country. Socialization continues throughout life. The new student, the army recruit, the young honeymooners—all become socialized as they enter their new roles.

Socialization is the process by which we gain the knowledge, skills, and dispositions that make us more or less able members of society. As we acquire the culture of our society and its subgroups, we learn the recognized social positions as well as the habits, beliefs, attitudes, and motives that enable us to perform satisfactorily the expected roles.

GALLERIES OF WITNESSES

Social rules constrain our ability to change in two fundamental ways. One is the control that others have over us through their rewards and punishments for our good or bad behavior. The second way—to be discussed in the next section of this chapter—is when these rules have been taken into ourselves, become part of our personality, become "internalized," as we say.

From the very first instance of a parent's saying, "You ought to be ashamed of yourself," the child can recognize that approval brings nurturance, relief, pleasure, and exhilaration; conversely, disapproval brings withdrawal of support, punishment, and the resulting anxiety and fear. Humans develop a powerful learned motive to "do right" in terms of others' standards and expectations. *Shame* is the customary term to describe the unhappiness we feel when we fail to live up to what others expect.

A few years ago, the *New York Times* carried a full-page advertisement for *People* magazine. The heading for the ad was "You're never too young to learn that winning isn't everything. It's the only thing." The text was about children's beauty contests:

> The competition was very stiff. There was Tina, a veteran with three hundred beauty contest trophies to her credit, and Trissy, who mesmerized the judges of the talent show with her hula. But in the end, three-year-old Kendall blew away sixty of the country's top tots and walked off with the gold.

There were accompanying photographs of the trio of three-year-olds, the winner with an armload of flowers and a crown.

On another occasion, the writer Roger Simon was doing research for his article "Winners, Losers—Each a Miss America." He went to interview the 1976 Miss Wisconsin finalist, the final step before Atlantic City. The eight losers ran off-stage and were led to a room where they could watch the victor on television. They were still in their evening gowns. "'I just feel bad for my town,' one said, 'I feel I let them down; I feel I let all the people down.' Another said, 'I don't know how I will face the people who came here to see me; I am dreading the moment.'"

The galleries of people who matter to us are populated by our family, earlier friends, great figures in history, distant heroes, ancestral spirits (in some cultures they are very much around and are fed in the kitchen corner every day), descendants yet to be born, God (or gods).

A son in the early stages of his career spreads his trophies at his parents' feet. Later, when they are gone, he thinks, "If my mother and father could only see me now." Another person—a daughter perhaps—may be unconcerned about her parents' judgments of her, but cares profoundly about what her descendants will say about her one hundred years hence.

A best-selling nonfiction author, unimpressed by the fact that more than two million copies of the paperback edition of his book had been sold, asked me instead, "Are the professors at Yale reading it?" Michael Jackson, famous for his 1982 pop music album *Thriller,* which sold twenty-four million copies and broke all records, says, "For the first time in my life I feel I have achieved something; I'm in the *Guinness Book of Records.*" In a television documentary show on an American monastery, a monk says, "I hope God appreciates what I am doing for him." A cartoon portrays a family sitting in the living room watching an evening television newscast: "Good evening, this is 'GuideLine' and here is today's list of standards against which you should measure your performance."

As we develop, certain people become particularly important to us: mother, father, siblings, male and female friends, teachers, loved ones, spouse, children, employers, and so on. We try to live up to the standards most of them set for us. But some are negative models, and we avoid being like them or following their dictates. Some may have a pervasive influence that extends into most sectors of our lives; others have only local or specific influence, such as a doubles partner in a tennis match. Some are stable through life—indeed, inescapable, a "life convoy" as the psychologist Robert L. Kahn calls them.

These social frames of reference, these galleries of "significant others," are unique for each of us. They are like fingerprints: no two are the same. We may share some figures in common, but we each create our own idiosyncratic world of people who matter to us. A friend reported that one year she happened to be a guest, among 150 others, of the French consulate for a fashion show. Amid the French lilacs, the 1940s music, the food and drink, and all the background, she heard one person say to another, "*Everyone* is here," though she knew only two people. Later that year, at the seventy-fifth anniversary party (another 150 guests) of a national social welfare organization in which my friend was active, one person said, "*Everyone* is here," and she knew all of them.

INTERNALIZED STANDARDS

As I noted, we are also constrained in our actions by rules we have internalized, so that no one else has to enforce them. Research on child development shows that, from about age two on, the standards of people who are important in a child's life have been incorporated into the child's personality as internalized guides to his or her performance. Children will experience an uncomfortable emotion, usually called "guilt," when they see they have failed to meet an internalized standard.

The *New Yorker* cartoonist Saul Steinberg draws a small dog walking along on its hind legs, thinking, in huge letters written in the sky: "Dog." Charles Barsotti draws an arctic wolf sitting on a snow-covered hill, thinking of itself as "Proud, independent, resourceful, cold." Mick Stevens draws "Roget's Brontosaurus," standing in an ancient tropical forest, thinking, "large, great, huge, considerable, bulky, voluminous, ample, massive, capacious, spacious, mighty, towering, monstrous."

However happy or sad, pleased or ashamed of itself a dog may appear to be, nature did not give dogs or other animals the ability to reflect upon themselves, to have images of what they are and what they are doing. The lizard lying on a flat rock in the sun may be feeling the heat, but it is not pondering the fact that it is lying on that rock in the sun. That ability is uniquely human.

Of all the other animals, chimpanzees come the closest to humans intellectually. In laboratory experiments, a chimp can recognize itself in a mirror and respond reflexively by touching a black spot on its forehead seen in the mirror. But monkeys, like dogs, attack the mirror as if it were another animal, or avoid it or ignore it. Human infants as they mature reach the age (about a year old) when, like the chimpanzee, they can touch the forehead spot in the mirror and, some time later, touch the same spot on their own foreheads. Then they go on to develop a sense of self. The five-year-old boy creating a self-portrait at school faithfully shows his strawberry blond hair and gray-green eyes.

Our unique capacity to see ourselves in action—in the past and in the future as well as the present—to judge and evaluate ourselves, is one of the sources of our feeling good or bad when we win or lose. We have our self-images in action and afterward, and we ask, "Did I do enough?" "Did I do it right?" Throughout our lives, we orient our behavior toward the preservation of our self-respect. We take into account not only what others think of us, but what we think of ourselves.

The internalization of standards may begin after the first year of life but it continues long afterward. Athletes are trained to create images of their own performance and taught to pay no attention to other contenders in a contest. The Olympic downhill skier Phil Meihre says, "You don't do it for your family or your country, you do it for yourself. I am more competitive with myself than anybody else." A woman running alone on an ocean beach at dawn, two young men making an overnight climb up Half Dome in Yosemite Park, a larger team on the other side of the earth climbing Mt. Everest—all have some kind of standard to be met, whether it is the distance of the run, the speed or height of the climb, or the emotional tone one is attempting to reach. Almost always, there are internal rules.

THE HUNT FOR LEGITIMACY

If I try to change, to find the right challenge, to set new levels of manageable difficulty, I usually have to free myself from some of the old rules I have lived by. If they are deeply internalized, they will be hard, even impossible, to shake off. If they lie only at the surface of my personality, it will be easier. Easiest of all is when I have been following the rules for the sake of conformity, but never adopted them as my own personal standards.

Whatever the level of difficulty may be, my change is helped along by finding new people or groups who approve of my new plans, and by avoiding those who are critical of what I now want to do. Let us consider the first of these, the hunt for legitimacy.

I think of an event I was told about linked to the famous Kinsey report (1948) on male sexual behavior, which presented a large amount of interview and questionnaire survey data on frequency and type of sexual practice. At the time, there was a vacuum of systematic knowledge about sexual behavior in the United States. A forty-year-old fruit and vegetable vendor came into a graduate student's Quonset hut apartment. Spying a copy of the Kinsey volume on the table, he said, "Ah, there's the book." He picked it up, found a particular page, and, pointing to a line in a table of numbers, said with obvious relief, "Here, that's me."

We search for approval before, during, and after we make a change. We want people to agree that it is correct to change, and that our new goal or our new behavior is acceptable. Our changes need validation by others. Often we can change without needing new reference groups or significant others; the change is within the current range of tolerance. At other times, we hunt for people who like what we are doing. We need a new legitimizing group or person.

Sometimes the change can be made just in our mind. Most New Year's resolutions are self-imposed standards that are not obvious or even apparent to the outside. These are secret new plans and can be legitimized by secret reference groups. Significant others fade away as a checkpoint and new figures take their places, without any overt behavior on our part. We have changed some of the portraits in our secret gallery of witnesses without anyone else knowing.

As we grow up, we gain freedom from the controls of our early reference groups as we meet, or hear or read about, new groups and new standards. We see that we can find new sources of approval—whether real or only in our minds—and discard significant others of earlier times.

We can look for standards that suit our changed position and desires. Social norms permit us to segregate by age, level of competence, body weight, gender—even by disability type (blind golfer tournaments, wheelchair races for the elderly, sheltered occupational workshops for the handicapped). Our lowered aspirations as athletes, for instance, can be legitimized by shifting to a new, older age group as a point of comparison. A professor who is a famous softball pitcher in a university and town league said to me that for the first time in many years he had lost two games this year. Conceding that this was the worst season he had had for a long time, he added, "I was thinking that I had been pitching softball for 50 years, and that was not a bad season for someone who is 63."

Similarly, a man who bought a stationary exercise bike for aerobics had to decide on the level of performance right for him. Since the standards in the brochure that came with the bike were based on men in Finland, who tend to be lean and healthy compared with the rest of the world, he set his level of aspiration at what the brochure indicated was "good" for his age, thinking that this would count as "excellent" in the United States.

Scholars, artists, and others who live around the edges of the main society may have to create the groups that anchor them and provide approval. Consider these exotic interests and activities of three scholars in the late Ming dynasty (seventeenth century) in China: "See fish swim in pond," wrote Feng Mengzhen; "Enjoy wrinkled rocks"; "See mother-in-law and ask about her health"; "Entertain young concubines." Chen Jiru said:

My fond interests: Studio. Clean table for painting. Cool breeze
and beautiful moon. Vase of flowers. Tea, bamboo shoots,
oranges and tangerines all in season. Amid mountains and rivers.
The host not being formal. Stretching under the sun. Famous
incense as offering. Research. Peace in the world. Talking to high
monks in the snow. Having strange rocks and bronzes by my side.
Getting up from sleep. Recovering from sickness. Freely display-
ing objects but slowly putting them away.

And Li Rihua wrote: "All I want is that in my whole life I have
white rice to eat, fish for soup, good wine and fine tea to drink,
and in my home ten thousand volumes of books and a thousand
stone rubbings. I want to not have to go out all year or to see any
vulgar person that someone tries to introduce to me."

In describing the way of life of these scholars, the Asia Society
galleries (in New York City) noted that their motivation was éli-
tist; and that in order to pursue their goals and avoid the dangers
of their contemporary society, they created for themselves a
unique community with common interests, which was crucial for
their survival.

The author Ronald Sukenick describes how authors deal with
the fact that they are "not recognized," as either a commercial or
a political success. They create counterculture groups (some
probably exist in all societies). Authors usually find some meeting place—"writers' bars"—where they can bond together. The
special writers' group gives the newcomer a culture, a set of standards, approval, and even prestige. Managing the failure to be
recognized involves rejecting the goals of the dominant culture
and lengthening timetables to allow for future recognition by the
right audience. According to Sukenick, the acceptable career
becomes that of a "'misunderstood genius working obscurely in
the garret. . . .' The first book was not to be an easy success."

If our hunt for a reference group is failing, we may be able to
move forward or backward in time. Franklin Baumer, a Yale history professor, once said that he was living in the wrong century,
and would have preferred to live in the Age of Enlightenment.
Robert Crane, once head of the international sales division of
Coca-Cola, wished he had lived in the first decade of the twentieth century. These successful men felt that their beliefs, achieve-

ments, and standards were from a bygone era, and that the reference groups whose styles of life and opinions they valued had disappeared from the human scene.

Robert Wilson is a sociologist who studies the arts and literature. His research on poets reveals how they can write poetry without any recognition or reward from their friends or peers, and even in the face of negative criticism about the value of their work. The poets believe that the generations still to be born will say that they were great poets even though rejected in their own lifetimes. They also travel through time into the past, to significant others who are dead. It is as if a poet were to think, "If Shelley were alive today he would appreciate my work."

Most modern complex societies are rich in possible sources of support when we are making a change. There has been an unprecedented emergence of social groups designed to provide support to those who are seeking to change. Over 15,000,000 Americans of all kinds are involved in nearly 500,000 organized groups of this nature. The fact is that many people at any given time must be looking for others like themselves, hungry to talk, wanting affirmation that what they are doing is right. When these seekers find each other, we frequently hear, "I am so glad to find you, to talk with you. I thought I was the only one with this experience."

There is a national organization for almost every conceivable personality change, from Alcoholics Anonymous to Transactional Analysis and Transcendental Meditation. Not many years ago, membership in such groups was stigmatizing: one often, for instance, kept silent about membership in A.A. But the stigma of membership is lessening, and these groups are increasingly tolerated and relied on by the larger society.

Many books describe these "self-help" groups. For example, *Becoming an Ex* (1988) by Helen Fuchs Ebaugh (an ex-nun herself), reports on ex-convicts, ex-alcoholics, divorcées, mothers without custody of their children, ex-doctors, ex-cops, among others. There are Recovery, Inc., for former mental patients; Parents Anonymous, for parents of abused children; Debtors Anonymous, for people in debt; and groups concerned with adopting children, giving up tobacco, alcohol, other drugs, and overeating, with becoming vegetarians, re-entering the labor force, psychic healing, and euthanasia.

I believe that those who are losing in their careers—either topping out or actually downwardly mobile—have the hardest time of all. They may try to deal with such loss by changing goals or lowering aspirations, dreaming of a more distant future, or experimenting with new behavior, but society is not set up to support them.

Hendrik Hertzberg, writing in *Esquire,* quotes from Christopher Mathews, administrative assistant to former U.S. Speaker of the House "Tip" O'Neill:

> "You have to win every time or you lose everything. It's like that Hitchcock movie where the guy has to get his cigarette lighter to light twenty times in a row or they'll cut his finger off. Only in politics they cut off something more serious." No one wants to be an ex-congressman, one of the walking dead who haunt the Hill. "When you're a member, they give you respect," says one who isn't anymore. "The minute you lose, you owe it all back. It turns out they only lent it to you. My God, the way they look at you when you've lost. The way they *don't* look at you."

Some of us find a solution by going back to the standards of our earlier years. Studies of business managers show how some aspire to the highest career achievement and do not consider themselves successful until they get to the top jobs. Others measure their success by how far they have progressed from starting jobs, and have as their points of reference those persons they knew at that time. Generally, as the managers grow older and begin to realize that they have reached the limit of their achievement, they are more likely to think in terms of the progress they have made over the years. In deciding what is "doing enough," they increasingly use the norms of people who were influential when they were starting out; and by age forty-five, they tend to be strongly "anchored downward."

We may, like artists, writers, and poets, create a new reference group whose members share our experience. The sociologist and career expert Robert Faulkner describes symphony orchestra musicians in second-rank orchestras as they find new performance standards with which to evaluate themselves. The musicians are encouraged to emphasize the good points of their current position, while belittling other possible career lines. They confirm each other's views about "the hazards, injustices, difficulties, and politics of going higher in the organizational ranks." They spare each other criticism for not having climbed fast or far enough. They "confess relief that their major career speculations and fears are now put to rest."

Organizations have customs to handle those who were stepped down in grade or lost in competition with other persons in the organization. Usually they are moved to a different department, or there is an arrangement for early retirement or a deal made with another firm to provide a position. This widespread process protects the organization from internal conflict but does little to help the employee find the new groups that will provide support for such a change.

What is missing are clubs for the losers. In one way, we have them—among the array of social clubs and civic and church groups to which most of us belong—but they do not go by that name, and levels of career achievement are hardly discussed in such groups. The rare "losers' club" seems to be located among the artists and authors who, as I said earlier, develop their own subculture of support while being judged failures by the more general social standards. But this is not quite the real thing, because these people do not consider themselves failures. The theologian William James Tilley described the case (in 1889) of a society in Paris composed of dramatic authors. To be eligible for membership, the dramatists must have had a play produced that had been rejected by the critics and the public: "An eminent dramatist is selected as chairman and holds the post for three months. His election generally follows close upon a splendid failure." There are monthly dinners, and these "are said to be extraordinarily hilarious."

We are not encouraged to talk about the experience of failure. But what is the purpose of keeping it quiet? Do the classic American values of the work ethic and career achievement need to be protected from examination? Consider how different it would be if workers in each occupation formed social groups in which membership was determined by public recognition that they had topped out in their work, and might even sink to lower levels during the rest of their working lives. These groups would be especially helpful in hard economic times, with so many "reductions in force," "out placements," and "early retirements." Can we visualize a national system of losers' clubs in which men and women sit around and talk about it being "all over," about how good it feels, how lucky they are that they can now go on to other things in life?

AVOIDING COMPARISONS

We want to keep ourselves safe from the intrusion of norms and rules that make us feel bad. We protect ourselves in some simple ways, one of which is to exclude others from our attention. The way this process operates is demonstrated in some unusual research in the psychological laboratory of the late Harry Helson, who studied the smallest recognizeable difference in the weight of things. Usually the participants in an experiment are presented with ten objects—balls or blocks or cylinders—very similar in weight and asked to array them from heaviest to lightest. Most people try to find the heaviest and the lightest and to set them at either end, as end points, creating a frame of reference. Then they try to discriminate between the remaining objects and place them in order.

In one variant of this experiment, a heavy suitcase is made to fall off a shelf. The participant is asked to help by picking it up and replacing it on the shelf, and then to continue with the judgment of the weights. Picking up the heavy suitcase does not affect the judgment of the smaller objects. It is too far off the scale to become part of the participant's frame of reference.

Where money is concerned, large differences in wealth between ourselves and others do not engage us. Most of us who work in large organizations do not know the differences in salaries beyond our immediate range. Orderlies in hospitals compare their income with that of a nurse but not of a doctor. Millions watch "Lifestyles of the Rich and Famous" on television with interest but without envy. In the magazine *Homes*

International, the houses portrayed are expensive and elegant, and few readers would be able to buy them. The main emotion one feels in looking through the magazine is not so much envy but curiosity (and perhaps daydreams), without personal impact. Similarly, as one woman said to me, idly leafing through *Town and Country,* "It's like an ordinary tennis player watching Wimbledon; it doesn't stir you up."

National surveys in the United States report that people with average incomes consider $100,000 "rich," while the more wealthy would not feel rich unless they had at least $1,000,000. Meanwhile, poor Hispanic immigrants living in Los Angeles refer to their barrios as "paradiso," comparing their present situation with the dirt huts, dirt roads, and lack of plumbing in their home countries.

There are in the world about 500 yachts that are more than 100 feet long. This is one frame of reference, but we can see at once that there can also be a group of owners of yachts over 300 feet, or even a few that are over 400 feet; and so it goes to the last two yachts—the largest and the second largest in the world. A man who has commissioned the building of a 150-foot yacht is now caught up in a bigger game.

Sometimes we find it hard to avoid the unwanted, intrusive challenges. A man who was trying to leave behind him the goals of wealth and fame recalled for me how some years ago he was caught in a storm of ambition, a short-lived state brought on by a week of accidental exposure to the very "life styles of the rich and famous" he was trying to reject. Some of the events were: perusing magazine articles on the U.S. Virgin Islands, on Anguilla and St. Martin, on Cat Cay; having lunch with an editor friend who reported that the best-selling novelist Andrew Greeley had received $1.8 million for a new book; viewing on television a rerun of the film *Diamonds Are Forever;* having a close friend profiled in *Newsweek.*

And the actress Mary Louise Wilson writes about being unemployed:

> The Sunday paper ought to be sedulously avoided in these periods; it is a letter from the enemy. But when you see those thick,

delicious-looking slabs being snatched from the newsstands like hot cross buns, it is just too hard to walk on by. Back home, trembling fingers turn to the entertainment pages, where you read about this play and that opening and examine the size of your peers' billing and the next thing you know you are stomping around the apartment in a rage, screaming about no-talents and praying for box-office disaster.

Some years ago, a man sold his business for $10 million and moved to Florida to start a new life style, only to run into a group of even wealthier neighbors with private plane safaris to Kenya, homes in Nassau, and much more. He said he would have been happier if he had never moved to the Gold Coast. There is, too, the familiar case of the top high school student who, after winning all scholastic honors and becoming class president, enters the freshman class at Stanford, and on the first day of classes finds a room full of people just like himself or herself. You win, you move up into a new frame of reference, and you start over again, probably near the middle or the bottom of the ladder among your new peers. It is like picking up the heavy suitcase, and this time it registers.

It is hardest to put family standards and comparisons behind us. A 1986 *Boston Globe* photo shows the DiMaggio brothers—Vince, Dom, and Joe—posing prior to an Old-Timers' game at Fenway Park in May. Vince once said, "I guess no matter what I do, I'll always be under Joe's shadow. He was one hell of a star, and I was just an ordinary star." And Gregory Hemingway, one of Ernest Hemingway's three sons, describes his lifelong attempt to put his father's standards behind him:

> I had an idea that if you slipped up at all, if you made any mistake, he was on you—for your own good. As a result, I had so little confidence that I was afraid to try anything, to fail. . . . The son of a bitch overpowered us. . . . He was so competent. He was so thoughtful. He was so this. He was so that.

We are usually content with our set of standards unless we keep running into other people who tell us the standards are wrong. How do we avoid these intrusions? Mayors of small villages are chiefs on their own turf; but at the state conventions of mayors, they often wish they had stayed home. Maybe next year they do. Some people avoid reading specialty magazines in their own areas of interest, such as *Gourmet, Tennis,* and *Fortune,* to avoid exposure to the highest-level comparison groups, although they avidly consume other magazines.

Sometimes we block out information about the achievements of others our age, not reading the works of great artists or biographies of great men and women because they impinge on our own sense of winning and losing. At age thirty-five one could be unhappy reading the special issues of *Esquire* on the United States leaders who are still under forty. But in our fifties, when most of our cards in life have been turned face up, we can read the biographies with interest and peace.

We reinforce our own standards of what it means to be successful by avoiding comparisons with higher standards, and comparing ours with those that are less demanding. In 1950 the sociologists Robert K. Merton and Alice Kitt (now Rossi) developed Samuel Stouffer's sociological concept of "relative deprivation" to explain the fact that less well educated soldiers were the happiest with their status in the military. Instead of seeing themselves as doing poorly compared with the better-educated and higher-ranking soldiers, those with less schooling compared themselves with their peers in civilian life and saw that they were reasonably well off.

Relative deprivation is explicit in the cynical definitions of happiness by Ambrose Bierce: "an agreeable sensation arising from contemplating the misery of another"; and by Russell Baker in his article "On Top in Wampum":

> We vacationed on historic Wampum Island. Everybody felt superior. The year-rounders felt superior to the summer people, who felt superior to the one-month renters, who felt superior to the "day-trippers" . . . People with private planes felt superior to people using the airlines, and those with private jets felt superior to those with propeller planes.

Reunions can be dangerous for people who have put behind them the standards of their family and their high school or college peer group. A teenage high school boy may have wished he could have been out of a social group and been a loner, free of the goal of popularity, rather than always on the margin trying to get in. Once having graduated, he could avoid situations that resurrected the norms and expectations of this youthful group. It is those who were happy and successful in high school and college who go to the reunions: the class presidents, the team captains, the cheerleaders, the prom queens. The unpopular misfit who later becomes successful rarely goes back.

We have to make our stand. A man of considerable worldly achievements once said to me in a superior tone, "Have you ever done anything really superb in your life?" I picked up this "heavy suitcase" and hefted it for a moment. I thought about a singer in Guatemala who was quite content with her performance, as were her family, her manager, and her local Guatemala City audience, and who turned down a tryout in New York City. I thought about the traveler in a science fiction story who is on an outlying planet in the other side of the galaxy. With an hour or two to spare, he drops by a nightclub where a nonhuman pop singer seems to be a great favorite with her audience: "She seemed to be happy and well-known in her corner of the galaxy." I put the suitcase back down, unmoved by its weight, and said, "Yes, of course I have—and so has everyone, in their own corners of the galaxy."

III

Keeping Up the Challenge

7

The Sequence of
Transformation

Of the four ways we deal
with success and failure, changing our behavior is the most primitive and is a method we share with other animals. Because it has been the subject of thousands of studies by psychologists, called "human learning," it is the best understood of our methods and needs no review or discussion in this book. Distinctively human, however, is our ability to alter timetables, levels of aspiration, and goals after success or failure, as I shall discuss in the three final chapters.

Before I move on to these topics, though, I shall make a brief analysis of both the sequence we tend to follow in making these changes, and how it differs following a loss or a win.

AFTER LOSING

In dealing with losses, we start by changing behavior. After a losing episode, the most direct method of dealing with the achievement gap is to work harder, increasing the effort applied to the same action. Sometimes this works. Sometimes it does not, especially when we try to force something to happen, like the child who unwittingly puts a key upside down into a lock and tries to get it all the way in by pushing harder and harder.

Many of us are trained as children to believe that hard work is the way to success; that the effort and time we spend on a task is the best single predictor of our accomplishment. Working harder seems a simple and straightforward solution. One man said to me, "I think a lot of people, including me, adopt the 'work harder' strategy. In my case it's partially due to ambiguity and insecurity; if I am working, that's all I can do and so I don't need to worry about other things. I think many people work hard for similar reasons; it's the easiest thing to do!" Others are trained to "work smart" and to look for a better way; indeed, some are "always looking for an angle," believing that there always is an easier and better way.

In trying to find a better way, our actions range from methodical and careful search to the frenetic actions of Phil Silvers's television character Sergeant Bilko in "You'll Never Get Rich," as he keeps devising new schemes to make money while in the army. Eventually we may reach the point where we see we may lose no matter what we do. Then, just before accepting the inevitable, some people start a wild and irrational search for new ways to deal with the impossible situation. They make desperate moves, resigning abruptly from a career, plunging into the stock market, trying to set up a love affair, making radical health habit changes. This is the "last chance syndrome": the nearly busted crap shooter putting everything he owns on the line for one last pass; the gold miner looking for the big strike in dangerous country before he dies.

The next step follows after trying out new behavior. For instance, a building contractor who cannot complete a home because of labor costs may try to change methods, finding new workmen or speedier ways of construction. Failing that, he will stretch out the time involved: we know that building or remodeling a house almost always takes longer than planned; it is the custom in the contracting business.

Later is the change in aspirations. A sixth-grade math teacher said to me that if the children did not learn what she wanted them to learn on a particular day, she felt she had failed. She would try a different method of teaching the same material. She would give them more time—an extra couple of days. If these methods did not work, she would lower her expectations and teach material that was less difficult. The goal of teaching the children math, however, stays put.

Only as a last resort do we give up our goals. A study of workers who were fired during an automobile manufacturing recession revealed that they overestimated their chances of re-employment and the wage they could get. Most of the workers reported turning down firm job offers because they thought they could do better, and continued to look for a better opportunity. In the end they had to give in and take a different job than what they wanted.

The sequence may be played out in the way organizations, like individuals, manage failure. Take, for example, the strategies used by several major banks in the United States and Europe when they realized they might not be repaid after making substantial loans to some third world countries. First, the banks changed their methods of encouraging repayment by giving the countries free technical aid and investing more money to help improve their production. When that did not work, they changed the timetable of repayment by extending the terms of the loan. When this, too, did not work out, they began to reduce the interest rate—in effect, lowering their hopes about how much money they would get back. And finally, some of the banks took the step of selling their loans at discounts to face value, just short of forgoing the loan completely and writing it off their books.

Obviously these sequences are not always followed. An alcoholic person who intends to quit drinking might at first engage in a timetable extension and put off quitting, saying, "Next week," or "On New Year's Day," or, "On my birthday." If this does not work, then one may adjust the level of aspiration, redefining "giving up alcohol" as cutting back to a few drinks. If unsuccessful, then the search begins for a new method, such as joining Alcoholics Anonymous and thus getting into a new group whose social constraints make the new behavior more likely.

Moreover, one may give up a goal at once or add a goal without much thought, without first trying out other methods. Another may focus on timetables only, expanding or contracting time expectations for achievement to a foolishly unrealistic point, dreaming of the future without ever actually getting anything done. Still another may concentrate only on behavior, unable to give up the goal or to settle for less or to be patient and wait. There is always individual variation around the basic sequence.

AFTER WINNING

When we win, our first reaction may be to check to see whether we actually have won, whether the winning event really happened—like the winner who looks at the lottery ticket fifty times to check the numbers; but then we move on to our plans. We shorten the timetable, we raise the level of aspiration, and we add new and different goals to our life plan.

Professor Gary Marx has, with some whimsy, described these changes after his success in his first years as a member of the faculty of Harvard University. He had a high salary, a long-term contract, a one-course teaching load, a corner office, a widely selling book, membership on national committees, top ratings as a teacher, fellowships, consultantships, meetings with the vice president of the United States and with cabinet secretaries: "In three short years. . . . I had already achieved far more than I ever intended or expected. . . . But I was too busy to think much about tenure in those early years. Besides, there was always the exception, and wasn't I on the fast track (as the list of achievements I also kept tucked away in the top drawer of my desk indicated)? . . . Who knows where it might lead?—an endowed chair, a deanship, a presidential appointment, honorary degrees, plenary addresses, editorships, more foreign translations, directorship of a research center, perhaps a best-selling novel and even a movie career."

Although changing behavior usually comes first in dealing with losing, it rarely appears in dealing with winning. Although we could raise the level of challenge after successful action by picking a more difficult means to reach our goal, we are unlikely to do so. Indeed, I think we are likely to do this almost only in play, as in a children's game, and even then as a last resort.

Children will work to master rolling a marble through a three-dimensional clear plastic maze, the purpose being to get the marble from one corner of the maze, through tunnels and holes, to the other diagonal corner. As experience brings success, a child's level of aspiration rises: going a longer distance without any errors, and then going the whole way without a mistake. A new goal is added: doing it backward. The timetable is shortened: the child goes faster and faster, speeding up the action to the limits of the effects of gravity, and then shakes the four-inch cube to make the marble move even faster. Only after all this has been accomplished does a child use harder methods, first standing on one leg, and finally doing it with eyes closed. After a while, perhaps several weeks, there is no growing edge left, and the maze is set aside.

HOW FAST DOES CHANGE HAPPEN?

Little is known about what personality characteristics, if any, may be associated with whether individuals are slow or fast to change. The rate may simply be the result of the situation one is in, or of differences in one's experience in dealing with events. Social psychologists note that stockbrokers believe amateur investors are reluctant to sell a stock when it begins to drop, and thus fail to minimize their losses. They point out that "mathematicians burn out by staking their careers on finding solutions to extremely difficult, perhaps insoluble problems. Ordinary people ruin their lives by persisting in efforts to maintain relationships with spouses, parents, or children in ways that may once have worked, but cannot work any longer."

Once we have decided to make a change, though, how fast we make it depends on how far into the sequence we have to go to find a solution that will establish our new level of difficulty. It gets harder for us, emotionally, as we move along the sequence. Changing behavior is one thing; shifting aspirations or goals, another. If, after a loss, we try out a new action and succeed at once, change is rapid. But it may take much longer to give up a goal that we see we will never reach. If the goal is fundamentally important in our lives, it may take years before we abandon and replace it.

Often we are slowed down by caution. Faced with a new plan we have created, we may be unsure that we are at the right level of difficulty, and perhaps dubious about the value of a particular new goal. We need time for a trial performance, a demonstration to ourselves, before we commit to action. The rehearsal can be done in thought or in action. I think that much of what goes on in dealing with winning and losing takes place in this tryout phase of transformation, whether imaginary or real, in thought or in action. We may have a new career plan that requires us to make it in New York City. We decide to "try New York City" for a few years and then go back to Columbus if we find the Big Apple too tough.

In a variation on the "sour grapes" fable, we may claim retrospectively that we were only trying something out and never meant it, even though we did. After being turned down on a proposal for a foundation grant, the applicant says, "I'm withdrawing the proposal. I didn't mean for you to really have it," or, "That was not the proposal I sent to you. That was just a question." In a kind of subjective rewriting of our ambitions to protect ourselves from the bad feeling of a loss, we say, "It wasn't the real thing. I was just fooling around."

Our own tryouts of our plans are not, of course, the same as "being tried out" by someone else—by a producer for a part in a play, by a team or a ball club, by a firm or a partner. The other people or institutions are trying out their own plans: namely, whether we might be good for the part in the musical comedy or solve the team's problem at third base. From our point of view, though, being tried out is a true win-or-lose event. These "tryouts" are the real thing: a win permits us to move ahead; a loss sends us back to waiting on tables or to the minor leagues.

The slowdowns caused by our trying things out are counterbalanced by the occasions when, following winning or losing, we change so rapidly that we are surprised and puzzled. We think,

"How can it be so easy for me to accept this and to fit it into my life?" To an observer we might appear very flexible, perhaps too flexible, as if what we had been doing before never meant much to us.

Close study of such instances reveals that they are part of a longer process: We believe that we are succeeding or failing in reaching a particular goal. We make numerous small concessions or advances; we make twenty or thirty small but incremental changes along the way. Perhaps we are not really aware of them; perhaps we justify them away, one by one, without realizing that they are cumulative. In anticipation of failure, we create an "escape plan" for what to do next if we lose. In expectation of winning, we create a plan for the next advance. Then, when success or failure actually occurs, we find we have already dealt with it.

8

Changing
Timetables

Scholars who study the meaning of time say it is likely to be represented by one of three central images: as a line, as a wheel, or as a pendulum. Time can go on and on; it can go round and round; it can go back and forth. Regardless of which image is dominant in a particular culture, all cultures mark small units of time to produce calendars and schedules. These help to link people in a society and are the basis for socially shared timetables, which in turn are the foundation of social norms and expectations about what we should do within a particular period.

Shortening or extending our timetables for achievement in accordance with how well we are doing is a distinctive human characteristic. After, perhaps, attempting a change in behavior, this is the first of the three other modes of dealing with winning and losing, and the easiest to use. In resetting levels of difficulty, we can shrink time or stretch it in our minds, in accord with our successes and failures.

Changing timetables, though, is a human ability that takes a while to acquire. Steven L. Klineberg, a social psychologist, writes that "from all appearances, the newborn infant lacks any awareness whatsoever of the flow of time. [The child] is essentially in an ever succeeding series of present moments. . . . Lacking imagery of any sort . . . [the child] remains as yet unaware of the qualities of the time that govern . . . existence."

Young children, just after infancy, focus on the ongoing action, a motivational state that psychologists describe as a "flow experience." Young children are unable to change timetables in response to winning and losing. A young child's impatience, the inability to delay and defer, explains the child's primitive search for alternative methods to achieve the desired goal, at the desired level, right now.

As we grow up and learn to regulate our actions according to what time it is—or will be, or was—individual differences appear. Some of us are more future-oriented than others. We spend a lot of time thinking about what we are going to become. A friend said, "I wish I could live longer, so I could be perfect when I die." But someone else might say, "I don't give much thought to the kind of person I will be. I just take life as it comes."

We differ in how far into the future we plan. Some will say, "There is no yesterday"; others, "There is no tomorrow"; and still others, "There is no elsewhere—only here and now." One woman said, "I'm a moment person. I don't have plans or schedules or timetables." One man ran through life with his mind always ten years ahead: "I've spent forty years living ten years in the future, and I just want one year of living in the present." Another woman said her timetable is in terms of several lifetimes of reincarnations, perhaps a thousand years apart.

Some years ago, a friend met in Washington with the business and economics reporter for the *New York Times* in order to invite him to spend a year as a visiting scholar at a leading research institute. His salary would be covered, and he would have the time to write a book. He responded by saying that when he got up in the morning he had to deliver twelve hundred words to the newspaper by noon, and another six hundred words by late afternoon. But when the day was finished, his work was done. There was nothing to carry forward into tomorrow. For him, "The idea of taking a year and having to write a book is one of the most frightening things I can think of." Thinking of the social scientists who were the usual visiting scholars, my friend could only reply, "The idea of having to get up in the morning and having to produce twelve hundred printable words by noon is the most frightening thing they could think of."

SOCIAL AND PERSONAL TIMETABLES

Throughout our lives, social rules regulate our freedom to change timetables. Society has a stake not only in what we want and how we go after it, but also in how quickly or slowly we get there. There are four kinds of social timetables specifying how quickly we should achieve something; the age at which we should achieve it; how long we should stay in a particular role or situation; and at what age we should enter and leave a role.

In the first timetable—how quickly we should accomplish something—are the familiar social norms about performance in the workplace. The whistle blows, the assembly line starts rolling, a certain performance is expected within a certain time. These norms are obviously different from one work role to another. Sometimes the social norms are clear and sharp: produce so many pieces per hour on the assembly line. Sometimes they are fuzzy and soft and open to individual differences in application: businessmen who must deal with "real problems in a real time framework" ridicule the indefinite time horizon of professors.

The second kind of timetable contains the rules about performance and age. It specifies achievements such as being toilet-trained by age two, being able to read by age five or six, or being out of secondary school by age seventeen to eighteen. Research in lifespan development charts the shared expectations for the time of major life achievements in work (reaching the top in one's job) and family (when a woman will bear her last child).

Robert K. Merton, the eminent sociologist cited earlier, has analyzed the third type of timetable, for what he terms "socially expected duration." These are the rules for how long we are expected to stay in certain social positions before moving on.

Familiar examples are the one-year position as an agency director, life tenure for an academic professor, the six-year term of a United States senator, prison sentences, time in a particular grade in military service between promotions, the training period as an apprentice before one becomes a master carpenter, and years on the job before one reaches seniority in a labor union.

The significance of "socially expected duration" shows up in everyday experience. There are timetables for promotion in corporations. If someone is promoted too fast, colleagues may conclude that something secret is going on between this person and the boss. The "lame duck" label is pinned on a person reaching the end of a stipulated term in office, signifying that he or she will soon be gone and thus is irrelevant to future plans. We run out of time, like a farmer in debt with a one-year limit to his loan, hoping to get the crop in and sold before the note is called and he faces a forced sale and bankruptcy.

The fourth kind of timetable specifies the age we should be before we can enter or leave a social role. It is sometimes said about candidates for various academic prizes that "she [or he] is distinguished enough, but just not old enough." The American and to some extent European, social expectations of retirement from one's career at age sixty-five are probably the best known of the exit timetables.

Our personal timetables are constructed somewhat differently because "real time" and "age" are essentially the same in marking the passage of time in our lives. Thus, our personal timetables can be defined by either one. We think, "I will reach the peak of my career when I'm fifty (in fifteen years)," but also, "I plan to live here only another three years (until I'm thirty-five)."

When we think about performance, we specify the amount of elapsed time—or the age—when we expect to reach our objective. As for duration, we think about how long it will be, or what age we will be, when we change from this state to the next: "How long should I be in this job?" "How long will this marriage last?" Certainly we get most of the content of our personal timetables from learning the timetables in our culture. We feel the social pressure to speed up or to slow down. We are told to do something faster, sooner, or younger in some areas, but in others are expected to go slower, do it later, or wait until we are older. But all of us have some parts of our lives that do not fit the social clock, that are "off time" in character.

CAREER ACHIEVEMENT

Both social and personal timetables are significant in work careers. All four timetables operate in careers: They may link advancement to performance in real time, as when an assistant professor at a university is given five years to produce published writing or research. They may relate advancement to performance by age—as in a Wall Street investment firm where if you have not become a partner by age forty you probably never will. They may also link career advancement to time spent in the job, as in the army where promotion is based on time in a particular grade. They may also link entry or exit to chronological age: that is, one achieves advancement or retirement simply by staying in a position until one has reached a certain age.

In many areas of work at a certain point—defined either by age or by real time spent in the career—one reaches the top in income, prestige, fame, power, or quality of work done. While these may vary in importance in a particular career—perhaps power in a political career, income in the legal profession, quality of work among scientists and artists, fame among performers— one finally hits the ceiling.

Three specific relationships between time and career achievement illustrate the different degrees of freedom possible depending upon the nature of our work: ordered versus episodic careers; relationship to age of peak performance; and relationship to the physical demands of the work.

Ordered versus Episodic Careers

Timetables for ordered careers are most likely to have clear steps of progression. A pure case is the military career of an enlisted man, which specifies an orderly sequence of advancement through positions for a twenty-year period. There are other ordered careers (that have looser timetables), such as the steady progression through a political party's ranks: elevation to prominence can come at an early age, late in life, or never at all.

Soon after beginning a job, workers acquire a fairly accurate idea of its career path and of the age when they will, on average, "top out." Master carpenters have learned their highest skills by age thirty; second-grade teachers, perhaps by thirty-five; and business executives, in their middle to late forties. In "dead-end" jobs, including semiskilled and unskilled manual occupations, there is no advance as a result of performance or time spent in the job: the end is in sight at the time of entry.

Of course, these timetables are based on two assumptions: that the occupation will last during one's lifetime and not change much. In our rapidly changing societies, both assumptions are weakened, and we may see a decline in the number of these timed and ordered careers. Meanwhile, the workers in these occupations are locked into social timetables that give them little freedom to change.

In episodic careers, on the other hand, the relationship between age, performance, and success is less predictable. In Wall Street in the corporate finance business, "at the beginning of the year, you don't know what deals you're going to do, who you're going to do them for, or what resources you're going to need." And so it is in politics, in show business, and sometimes in literary careers. If we plot lifetime distributions of income or prestige or power in such occupations, we find a looser association with age: no clear "achievement curves" here; society holds no timetable for these people.

Thus, in an episodic career, we are relatively free to construct and to change around our own personal timetables for achievement as a way of managing our wins and losses. Our personal plan may be complex or of the simplest kind. All it may contain is the point in our life by which the "lucky break" must occur. An aspiring young performer, seeking fame, says, "I am looking for a vehicle to lift me into stardom."

Age of Peak Performance

The second important relationship between timetable and career achievement is the age of greatest creativity. More than fifty years of research by social scientists has been analyzed by Dean Keith Simonton. The works of scientists or artists that are judged by their peers as most original and valuable are matched with the age at which these were produced. The results show creative output tends to rise fairly rapidly through the years to a definite peak, and afterward declines until productivity is about half the rate it was at the top. The age of peak performance varies by field, though:

> At one extreme, some fields are characterized by relatively early peaks, usually around the early 30s or even late 20s . . . , with somewhat steep descents thereafter, so that the output rate becomes less than one-quarter the maximum. This age-wise pattern apparently holds for such endeavors as lyric poetry, pure mathematics, and theoretical physics, for example. . . . At the contrary extreme, the typical trends in other endeavors may display a leisurely rise to a comparatively late peak, in the late 40s or even 50s chronologically, with a minimal if not largely absent drop-off afterward. This more elongated curve holds for such domains as novel writing, history, philosophy, medicine, and general scholarship, for instance.

Some fields—psychology, for instance—show age curves somewhere between these two, with a maximum output rate around age forty and then a notable but moderate decline.

These research studies have been criticized because they do not take into account other factors that may cause this age-achievement relationship. In science, for instance, the rapid growth of a field (such as high-speed computers) means that there are more young scientists than old, and hence more contributions will come from the younger age group. And scientists who die young make no contributions in later life, making it seem that less work is being done by older scientists, when in fact there are fewer of them. But even when these and other criticisms are taken into account, the relationships between age and achievement do hold up and, in fact, have been shown to exist for different cultures and in different historical periods.

The important point about personal timetables for achievement is that the relationships just described are averages for hundreds of separate creative individuals; individual careers will sometimes show substantial variation around the average peak. Thus, you can say, "Those facts about achievement may be true for most people, but they do not have to apply to me," leaving you free to shorten or lengthen your own timetable.

Physical Demands

Timetables for career achievement are also based on the physical demands of one's work, and here we are less free to make changes. Athletes and manual workers require strength, speed, and dexterity; philosophers and writers do not. The former's advance in career is affected more by biological aging than by any other factor. Some compensation for physical decline can be found in the skill and wisdom experience can bring, but this comes to an end. The seasoned ballplayer has "lost his step" or "can't get around on the fast ball," and the professional singer "can't reach the high notes any more."

Occupations with limited tenure—say, twenty years—also usually require skills that fade with age, such as certain police, fire, and civil service occupations. Here are some items from the description of the policeman's role: "A policeman . . . must climb bridges and buildings, like a steeplejack[,] . . . must stand up to gunfire, like an infantryman[,] . . . must keep fit, like an athlete[,] . . . does not flinch before the stares of the hostile, the bricks and bottles of the alienated, or the knives of the demented."

The sociologist Robert Faulkner, whose research on careers I mentioned earlier, shows that in many occupations job holders are "urged to recognize and face up to the career dilemmas of becoming occupationally and biologically older." He refers to studies of fashion models, professional fighters, lawyers, scientists, industrial executives, strippers, dancers, actors and actresses, teachers, engineers, and technical specialists. Comparing career paths in sports and in élite symphony orchestras, he gives a sharp demonstration of the effects of aging.

Professional hockey players, whose proficiency is correlated with youthful strength and resilience, must make it to a position with a top professional team in their twenties because their chances deteriorate sharply after that. Among those who have made it to the top, most will stay from one to three years, then return to the minor leagues, and gradually disappear from the occupation at a later age. For the others, the "superstars" who last, staying ten years in the top teams is not unusual. But, in contrast to both groups of athletes, symphony orchestra musicians, once they have made it to the top, are likely to stay there throughout their careers.

EARLY CLIMAXES AND LATE BLOOMERS

Two variations in work career achievements that sustain us as we change our own timetables are captured in the cases of early climaxes and late bloomers. I think that we use these points of reference mainly in dealing with losing, as we extend our timetables. The late bloomers give us courage to continue in a longer time frame. For the early-climax cases, we observe how they may suffer in later years, and thus have a reason to reject them as comparisons.

Some men and women reach their peak early in life—the early climax. For example, the late Italian novelist Alberto Moravia, was interviewed by several people about his first book, *Gli Indifferenti:*

INTERVIEWERS: Will you tell us something about it?

MORAVIA: What do you want to know? I started it in October 1925. I wrote a good deal of it in bed. . . . It was published in '29.

INTERVIEWERS: Was there much opposition to it? From the critics, that is? Or, even, from the reading public? . . .

MORAVIA: Oh. . . . No, there was no opposition to it at all. It was a great success. In fact, it was one of the greatest successes in all modern Italian literature. The greatest, actually; and I can say this with all modesty. There had never been anything like it. Certainly no book in the last fifty years has been greeted with such unanimous enthusiasm and excitement.

INTERVIEWERS: And you were quite young at the time.

MORAVIA: Twenty-one. There were articles in the papers, some of them running to five full columns. It was without precedent, the book's success. (*Pausing*) I may add that nothing approaching it has happened to me since—or, for that matter, to anyone else.

Achievements that come early in life, ahead of schedule, are in greater danger than most of being lost while one is still alive. One of Irwin Shaw's best-known stories, "The Eighty-Yard Run," describes the early fame that comes to a college football star unable to equal those achievements in the years that follow. Similarly, the writer Robert Lipsyte describes professional football players facing the fact that they must give up élite athletic careers. As one says, "It's a death experience." Lipsyte sees their youthful achievement as a bargain the athlete makes with a society that gives him a glorious half-life. He writes that the biggest loss is for the average pro—typically a black lineman from the South or West with neither a college degree nor a marketable nonfootball skill, but with significant knee and ankle damage that will give him increasing pain for the rest of his life. He is basically on his own. A player's wife says, "We put them beyond what they can stand, their image of themselves is so overblown they can't get back to where they want to go."

And the same happens, of course, in show business: Carrie Fisher, daughter of the superstars Eddie Fisher and Debbie Reynolds, and herself an actress and writer, described in an interview the dangers of the Hollywood fast track: "Two years ago, Ms. Fisher . . . whose films include 'Shampoo,' which began her career at age 16, the 'Star Wars' series, and 'Hannah and Her Sisters'—was in a drug rehabilitation clinic. . . . Drugs, both legal and illegal, had fueled her 12-year tear down celebrity's fast lane." She said, "'You live faster. You get there sooner. It was as good as it could get when I was born. I was world-weary at 20. I had unlimited access, money, fame and acceptance.'" The poet

Robert Browning writes: "She had a heart—how shall I say—too soon made glad."

Of course, we can lose things that we have not won but were born with: eyesight, good looks, family name, intelligence, strength—things we have taken for granted. We can lose things that we partly won and partly are ours through our growing older: pensions, promotions, inheritances. But most often we lose what we actually have won: a job, a home, money, friends, love, power, health, prestige, fame.

How much can we really keep of what we have won? Our money and possessions are always under attack, houses deteriorate, beauty fades, bodies weaken. Entropy governs what we have achieved; maintenance never ends. We continue to validate, to defend, to win again, to sustain what we have. The late, immensely successful songwriter Irving Berlin said, "The toughest thing about success is that you've got to keep on being a success"—the hardest of truths in lives with early climaxes.

There are exceptions, like Amelia Earhart and Albert Einstein, whose achievements endure. Instead of saying, "What have you done for me lately?" we can say, "If they never did another thing, their names will live in history." And in sports, if you are great enough—Ted Williams, Joe DiMaggio, Sugar Ray Robinson, Joe Louis—you are called "Champ" forever.

And also if you retire early. Greta Garbo was, from her twenties to her early thirties, one of Hollywood's greatest stars. At the age of thirty-six she retired from film making after one of her movies failed, in order not to lose her legendary status: "My legend is everything to me now. I would not sell it for life, happiness, or anyone. . . . As a matter of fact, I would even sacrifice my own life so as not to jeopardize it."

Some say the losing hardly matters—as in the saying, "Easy come, easy go." And, of course, Tennyson wrote, "'Tis better to have loved and lost, Than never to have loved at all." Still, most early-climax lives fit lines from the recent novel *Replay:*

"Well, all right!" Becher said from the stage, wiping the mouthpiece of his clarinet. "Now, this next one is really what the blues is most about. You see, there's some blues for folks ain't never had a thing, and that's a sad blues . . . but the saddest kind of blues is for them that's had everything they ever wanted and has lost it, and knows it won't come back no more. Ain't no sufferin' in this world worse than that; and that's the blues we call "I Had It But It's All Gone Now."

As we travel farther through the lifespan, and our dreams have not yet come true, we can take heart from the late bloomers. We think of the sweetness of success that might yet come—winning after you thought you had lost. We note the many authors, photographers, performers, actors, composers, whose work was not rewarded until long after it first became public. Abel Gance's 1927 film *Napoleon,* unnoticed when it first appeared, was resurrected for a 1981 film festival revival and acclaimed a masterpiece. Gance, then ninety-three years old, had a year of triumph before he died. Duke Ellington said, somewhere years ago, "Fate is being kind to me. Fate doesn't want me to be famous too young." A novelist, Helen Hooven Santmyer, finally cashed in her fifty-year effort at the age of eighty-eight. From her late thirties on, she had been writing a 1,344-page novel, "—*And Ladies of the Club*" (1982), about life in small-town Ohio, which was a best seller and chosen as a main selection of the Book-of-the-Month Club.

Winston Churchill is among the great cases of later life success (in his late sixties and early seventies)—but one of his contemporaries said this about him in his early years:

> As an administrator Winston Churchill has been cautious to excess and followed his chief war adviser, Admiral Lord Fisher, very closely[,] . . . no great or original stroke of genius need be expected from him in any place. . . . He reads only to prepare his speeches and has no other artistic tastes. But, on the other hand, he is easy of approach and his heart is in his work; he listens to everyone, even though he cannot grasp all that is said to him; in fine, he is an excellent subaltern: capable, industrious, and supremely courageous, but not a pathfinder or great leader of men.

And thus we can think of ourselves as the exceptions to whom rules do not apply. We say to ourselves, "I can work harder, find

a lucky break, get on the fast track, and be there ahead of time."
Or if we fail, we gradually change our self-image from being an
early achiever to being a late bloomer. We support our belief by
thinking of those who were different. Dancers point to the late
Margot Fonteyn; writers, to Daniel Defoe who wrote *Robinson
Crusoe* at age fifty-nine. Again, we can deny the average
timetable. "It may happen to them, but it's not going to happen
to me."

SPEEDUPS AND STRETCHOUTS

A friend said, "You can't compete with Father Time." But it is
clear to me that we do just this. By extending the time we allow
ourselves to fulfill our plans, we reduce the pressure and bring
the level of difficulty back to where we can manage it. By speeding up our timetables, we raise the level to where it is interesting,
satisfying, and challenging.

An author after a productive morning reduces, in her mind,
the time she expects she will need to finish the book. A young
minor-league pitcher, after turning in an exceptional performance, believes he may make it to the majors next year, not the
year after. The man getting a sign of warmth and affection from
the woman he loves decides to propose marriage sooner than he
had planned. After closing an extraordinary deal, the young Wall
Street investment banker, determined to become rich, sees her
goal within reach in three years, not the ten she has allowed.

Even in the plainest task, when things are going well, we speed
up what we are doing. Every fall, older winter residents head
south to Florida or to southern Texas along the Rio Grande.
Their automobiles are packed in the back seat, trunk, and on top
with gear, luggage, and household treasures; some pull a trailer
in addition. The goal may be to drive from New England to
Florida, and the timetable of three days calls for doing about 500
miles on each. But even these old people, with time on their
hands, will speed things up to give themselves a manageable
challenge. If the car is running well at 65 and 70 miles an hour,
the traffic is light, there are no accidents, and the road has been

improved going through the tunnel at Baltimore and getting around Washington, one of the two may say to the other, "Let's not stop at Fredericksburg. Let's go on to Richmond or Petersburg. Then on the second day, we can get to Savannah instead of Walterboro, and arrive the next noon."

In contrast, we slow down our timetables when we have seen that we do not have the capacity to reach our goal in the short run. The author finds ideas in the book to be more complex than expected; the pitcher needs more experience because the batters he now faces are better than ever; the woman being pursued must develop more trust in her relationship before marrying.

Often we need more time simply to let the consequences of our earlier actions run their course. In the Western world, the painter Paul Gauguin is the best known of the successful dropouts. When he left for Tahiti, he separated from his wife, telling her that his future fame would be his children's reward. They should be patient, he advised.

Often, too, we wait for beneficial changes in a world beyond our control—changes that increase our capacity or remove obstacles. In time, an injury will heal, medical research will produce a new wonder drug, the interest on funds in the retirement savings account will continue to grow, the color barrier to employment in a specific occupation will fall, an enemy of many years will die. We wait for a war to end: In the Second World War, as bomber pilots in the South Pacific and then later in occupation in Japan and Korea, we said, "Home Alive By '45"; then, "Golden Gate By '48"; and later, "It'll Be Nifty in 1950."

In 1987, the stock market crash in the United States was a major losing episode in the lives of many Americans. All four modes of management became engaged. Those who were hurt enough to feel that their entire future was wiped out transferred their money from stocks into savings accounts, giving up completely trying to "make a killing" in the stock market. Others lowered their aspirations and went back to an earlier life style, where in fact they had been just as happy as they were when the Dow Jones reached 2800 before the crash. Others changed their methods of investment—changing brokers, lowering the quality of the companies they invested in, taking bigger risks, buying puts, calls, futures, straddles—the "last chance syndrome" again. But still others changed their timetables for getting rich. "My buddies and I used to stand around in bars laughing during the bull market and say, 'Just give me five more years,'" recounts Bob Smith, a senior trader at Dean Witter. "Everybody figured, five more years like that and we would have enough money to get out. Now everybody says, 'Just give me seven more years . . . or ten.'"

And so it was in the crash of 1973–74, although then many had made their fortunes in the affluent years just past and had quit work ahead of schedule—quit their jobs or sold their businesses and retired early. Everything they had was lost. Back to work they went, with a much longer timetable now, stretching out far beyond what they had ever envisioned.

We might think that death puts the immutable and final constraint on our timetable stretchouts. But, no, we find another way. A study by Frank R. Westie of his fellow American sociologists found that about 40 percent expect to go down in history as being among the top ten leaders in their field of specialization. Since there are more than ten thousand sociologists in the United States and about twenty specialties in the field, being in the "top ten" in one of these means that there are only two hundred slots open for about four thousand sociologists. One out of twenty will win, and the other nineteen will fail. Comparing those who have been in the profession for more than twenty years with those who have just begun, Westie found no change in the proportion who have set this goal for themselves. The aspirations of the older sociologists have not lowered; instead, they have stretched out the timetable indefinitely. With only soft criteria for evaluating achievements, the day of reckoning can be postponed. With nothing powerful to contradict them, these scholars can go to their graves believing that posthumous evaluation of their work will place them in the "top 10."

Even better may be to believe in life beyond the grave. Raymond Chandler, the detective story writer, can call death *The Big Sleep*, but most Americans hold a belief in life after death. Four-fifths believe Heaven exists, and most of them expect to get there. Slaves in ancient Egypt, building the pyramids, believed that they, too, would have a full afterlife.

Most will agree that death always comes too soon. I think of the cartoon of the man who, looking up at his door to see the Grim Reaper who has just appeared, says, "Not now; I've got too much in the pipeline." But the timetable can extend into life after death, a life as real in the mind as is life on earth. What we could not achieve in this life will be ours in the next. Immortality of soul or spirit gives us more time—perhaps infinite time—to finish what we started and to get around to new and different lines of endeavor.

THE NEXT GENERATION

Living through the achievements of others in the next generation is a fundamental use of time to deal with our failures to achieve our goals. We stretch out our time frame to include their lives (and even the lives of their descendants), involve them in the pursuit of the goal that we have sought but never reached, and then succeed through their accomplishments.

This familiar human experience is best understood within the context of teamwork. Teaming up with others to combine capacities, share labor, and use complementary skills provides a powerful way to reach our shared goals. The family is an obvious case in point. One of the first institutions invented by humans, it is likely to be the last to go if civilization comes to an end. There is mutual aid toward a shared goal, with a division of labor according to resources and abilities. In the early period of European settlement of the United States, many frontier wives died in childbirth. Their husbands would marry again as soon as possible, often within a week after traveling to a larger village or town to find a single woman, who herself needed a man to help with her life. The events that men and women faced on the frontier in keeping themselves and their children alive could not be managed successfully alone.

Sometimes the reasons for teaming up are more personal and selfish than shared. Failing in their life ambitions and seeing no solution, countless women in small towns or villages, where they were born and raised, each found a way out by leaving with a traveling salesman, an athlete on a tour, a member of a band on a one-night stand, who came through town. Some have candidly admitted, "He was my ticket out of here."

In the simplest case, the child who holds off parents who want to help by shouting, "Me do it," will, on a different occasion when losing, cry, "Help me, help me." More complex is the crisis of great success or failure when we may team up with experts who have access to useful knowledge and are experienced in dealing with the particular crisis. Sociologists say that "a professional is a person who routinizes other people's crises"; and one counselor said, "My job is to take care of the first half hour of everything."

We may want to get off a losing team and move to a winning one, but find we are not free to do whatever we wish. Most of us, for some of the time, are stuck with teams that we either joined early or that society gave us. If we are on an unsuccessful team, we may try to help our teammates. Wanting them to try harder, we may work to motivate our partners. Better than exhortation to more effort, we look for outside trainers, teachers, and experts to help, try to increase capacity, to "work smart," to innovate within the limits of our team.

Sometimes we work through what might be called a "quasi-team." Those involved will gain from a success, or lose something in the failure, but what they actually win and lose is different. Familiar quasi-teams are trainers and athletes (the first textbook on training was written in Athens in 444 B.C.), teachers and students, masters and apprentices, parents (especially in immigrant families) and children, patrons and artists, mentors and protégés, power brokers and public officials, clergy and kings, directors and actors, agents and show business people, sponsors and candidates, caddies and golfers, and perhaps even jockeys and horses.

About a generation ago, two thirty-five-year-old professors at a university were competing for promotion to a tenured appointment, where only one could be promoted. The selection was made; and some months later, the loser drove to the city dump and committed suicide. A year later, the winner's mentor, the professor with whom he had studied and obtained his Ph.D.

degree, said to me with pride, "You know what killed —; my boy killed him. He was too tough for him." In the 1981 film *Chariots of Fire,* the Italian coach of the young English runner says, when the youth wins the big race, "I won—I've waited thirty years for this." It is said of the boxing trainer Angelo Dundee that after more than three decades and nine world championships, he is the best there is in aiding a fighter between rounds. In helping to produce the champions, he finds his achievement.

Sometimes we win or lose in what might be called "vicarious teams." We experience or realize an event through imaginative or sympathetic participation in the experience of another person. What kind of change can we make under such conditions, when we are wholly dependent on someone else's achievements? A baseball fan, for instance, makes virtually no contribution to the success of the team on the field other than cheering it on. The fan cannot advise, train, or teach the players.

Millions of people identify with celebrities, vicariously sharing their successes and failures, whether alone or as members of fan clubs. Many people identify with the heroes in the hard-boiled detective fiction of Raymond Chandler, Dashiell Hammett, Ian Fleming, and John D. MacDonald. Biographers live through their subjects—as James Boswell and Samuel Johnson, or Ernest Jones and Sigmund Freud.

In the early centuries of the Olympics, the athletes' native cities were fan clubs living through their victors. Winners were entitled to triumphal entries into their home cities in chariot processions, as today's victorious college or professional team returning to its home city is greeted by a crowd at the airport, train station, or bus depot.

Dealing with a win or a loss is usually harder on players or performers than on the people living through them, yet the vicarious experience must also be managed. When our team wins, the experience is close to, if not the same as, that of the players. It is said that when the Pittsburgh Steelers lose, the psychiatrists in their home city have more clients.

In living through others, we can manage success and failure much as we would if it were our own. We can change to another team or another celebrity (the fickle public), trying to catch a rising star. But the loyal fan does not jump around from one favorite to another. Instead we are patient, and shift our aspirations. We want our team to win, but we have to recalibrate each year: this year we will get out of the cellar; this year we will end up in the first division; some day we might win the pennant or even the World Series.

There is one type of goal we never have to give up, even if we ourselves are failing, because the quest will be carried on by others—team members of one kind or another—after we die. Consider, for example, a forty-year-old woman who has spent much of her life helping others. She writes to me:

> One of the organizations that I belong to is Ananda Marga. The members are idealists whose goals express their vision of a better world. They start with the "impossible dream" and take small steps, sometimes forward, sometimes backward, toward those goals. It is never a matter for them of scaling back their aspirations, because they will never compromise their goals and visions, and since they are not bound by a lifetime, or by a particular set of individuals, there is never the problem of running out of time. For example, one branch of Ananda Marga, AMURT, which is the relief branch, has for its goal that no one in the world will die of natural or man-made disasters. Though AMURT has done some impressive relief work in times of disaster, it certainly hasn't come close to that goal. And yet, the goal remains. But, for the short term implementing of projects, scaling back may be necessary for a time. I remember when Ananda Marga Women's Welfare Department was trying to purchase a building in New York City for its center. They wanted it in Manhattan, and they had a goal to have it by a certain year. They discovered that they didn't have the purchasing power to realize that goal. They had to instead buy a small apartment in Queens which they kept for maybe 3 years before they were able to buy their own building. And when they did buy their own building, it was in Queens and not Manhattan, because of financial limitations. But the goal will never be to stop here and be satisfied. The vision remains to open more centers, in more places over time.

The natural transfer of ambition to the next generation is, of course, from parent to child. Through the centuries, the relationship between parent and child in contemporary Western societies has changed from being a team to being a quasi-team. The child moves out of the family, geographically and socially. There are similarities between Angelo Dundee's training and launching a fighter into a career and a parent's training and launching a child into a career. The goals are more numerous and varied than winning fights, but the principles are the same. Just as the trainer must face the success or failure of his fighter, so the parent deals with the success or failure of the child, adapting aspirations to reality, shifting the emphasis on one or another goal, and often giving up earlier hopes for the child's achievements.

For some parents the primary purpose is to get all of their offspring onto socially acceptable paths—that none end in jail, that all are self-supporting, that all have jobs, that they are good citizens. These are strong achievements for low-income minority parents given the social hurdles they face in raising their children.

For others, the emphasis on upward mobility may predominate. The great waves of immigration to the United States in the decades just before and after 1900 created an almost ritual sacrifice of the parents as second-generation children moved out of the traditional family culture and into the new world. Children were encouraged and supported by their fathers and mothers to leave the old standards behind and take up the new and different, to make their way and be a success in the new society. If their children do not exceed them, many parents feel guilty, sensing that somehow they have failed their children or have done something wrong. Many children believe that their parents owe them a strong start in climbing higher up the ladder in their generation.

There may also be different individual and personal motives at work. A twenty-year-old mother of an illegitimate daughter says, "Maybe I'll put her on the stage and be famous that way." A man of small stature says to his three-year-old son of average size, "I hope you will be six-feet-two and weigh two-hundred and twenty pounds." A woman with good looks but not much else selected a handsome man to marry in order to produce a child who could be marketed in show business and provide a family income for her. (It worked: her daughter is a young movie star.)

We pass on unfulfilled ambitions to our children. In Arthur Miller's *Death of a Salesman*, Willie, the central figure, is sixty-three, and Biff, his oldest son, is thirty-three. The play starts with a flashback of Willie about forty-six and Biff about sixteen, when Willie had dreams of rising in the organization instead of staying just a salesman. When we pick up the story, he is out of money, has no savings; his car, house, and possessions are breaking down. Five weeks earlier, he was taken off salary and put on straight commission. Despite this forced retirement, he is continuing on his own. It is a day of reckoning; there are no more time extensions for his dream. Then he is really fired and requested not to be a representative for the company, even on commission. He had asked for a reappointment on a salaried basis, but there is no second chance.

Willie now lives through Biff. A glamour boy athlete in high school, Biff has become a drifter, and Willie must deal with the achievement gap created by his son's failure. His method is to extend the timetable for Biff, even though he is in his thirties and showing no promise. Ironically, the next-door neighbor's son, Bernard, whom Willie always rejected as the wrong model for his sons, becomes successful and forces Willie to see Biff's reality. Nonetheless, Willie creates in his mind still another time extension for Biff. At the end, Willie commits suicide in a simulated car accident to bring in $20,000 of insurance "for Biff," still trying to launch him in a successful career.

As it may be with father and son, so with mother and daughter. In Channelview, Texas, according to court records filed in nearby Houston, Wanda Webb Holloway, the organist at a Channelview church, tried to hire a killer to murder her neighbor, Verna Heath. (She was later convicted by a jury of solicitation of murder and sentenced to 15 years in prison.) Mrs. Holloway's purpose was to help her daughter, Shanna, win a cheerleading contest over Amber Heath, her neighbor's daughter. By having the girl's mother killed, Wanda Holloway thought she would cause so much grief that Amber would not be a threat to Shanna in the competition for next year's freshman cheerleading squad at the high school. Mrs. Holloway had been divorced for years, and her primary interests were her children and her church. "She was living her life through Shanna," her lawyer said. "Shanna's achievements were all she had, and it had become an obsession."

The challenge we pass on to our children may be grave—as were a Japanese executive's final thoughts, which he scrawled across seven pages of a pocket calendar in the last terrifying minutes aboard a Japan Air Lines jumbo jet before it crashed in August 1985:

> "I'm very sad, but I'm sure I won't make it," scribbled Hirotsugu Kawaguchi, 52. . . .
> As passengers frantically donned life jackets, Kawaguchi wrote sadly to his wife and three children: ". . . Be good to each other and work hard. Help your mother."
> To his son, Tsuyoshi, he wrote, "I'm counting on you."

Dealing with our children's wins and losses in areas in which they are carrying on our dreams is like managing these events in our own lives. We estimate their capacities—their intelligence, size, looks, health, energy—and set in our minds goals, levels of achievement, and timetables for them. Then we must deal with their success and failure—in school, on the playground and in sports, in morality and character, in friendships and popularity, in their choice of work and their career success, in their contributions as citizens, in their marriages, and in their children. Sometimes our children die before us, and in their death die our own dreams.

Usually over time we downgrade our expectations for our children because our early expectations exceed what is realistic, and maintaining them can be destructive. In the family, as in other quasi-teams, the parent can destroy the child by expecting too much, by bringing the child up too fast. Unrealistic expectations for children, the "superbaby" concept some parents hold, ruin many lives. As is obvious from Asian achievements, this is not just an American concept. Among élite Japanese families the term *Mama-gom* ("monster mother") denotes this pressure on the child.

At times parents underestimate their children's capabilities, perhaps knowing nothing about the sphere in which a child has extraordinary talents. Almost every child will go, more than once during childhood, beyond what the parents expected or hoped for. Some children, in fact, continue to succeed beyond their parents' expectations, giving the parents a life of vicarious victories which they follow with rising aspirations and perhaps dream of even more successes for their child.

In dealing with the winning and losing events in our children's lives, we are not as free as in other quasi-teams. Norms and rules for the family restrain our efforts. Angelo Dundee could get another fighter to train; the teacher finds a better pupil; the fan picks another celebrity to follow. Usually parents cannot switch teams when their children are losing—although in Iranian society in the past, if a man's own son did not look promising, he would adopt a more gifted boy. What often happens is that the most successful child is singled out as the carrier of parental ambition.

Living through children does have this advantage, however: we can stretch out the timetable for a child's attainments, and then shift to a grandchild. And beyond that grandchild are the next generations. In our fantasies, we can add new players almost indefinitely.

9

Changing Levels of Aspiration

Parents and guidance counselors advise high school seniors to apply to college at three levels of aspiration: their dream choice, their "fall-back school," and their realistic choice—the best school they actually expect to get into. Similarly, when college students are asked about the grade they expect in a course, they can distinguish between the best grade they believe they could get, the grade they are sure they will not fall below, and the grade they expect to receive.

We can think of these as the ideal, the minimum, and the realistic levels of expected achievement. The line between ideal aspirations, on the one side, and grand illusions, on the other, may be thin but it is there. It is the line between aspirations that have some chance of realization, and a reality-escaping fantasy. "I drink the wine of aspiration," writes John Galsworthy, "and the drug of illusion."

The ideal and the minimum are the "best case" and "worst case" scenarios. The realistic level usually is the level of just manageable difficulty. To achieve more requires a performance/

capacity ratio that is too demanding; below this level, we are underloaded.

DECIDING HOW MUCH IS ENOUGH

In our mobile society, many of us have had the experience of setting a price for selling our house or condominium. Drawing on the knowledge of a real estate agency, on information from friends, acquaintances, and newspapers, we set an ideal asking price, a minimum bottom price, and a price we expect to get. Similarly, in choosing the colleges we expect to be admitted to, we compare our SAT scores with the average SAT scores of the students admitted to various colleges, and select colleges whose students' scores match our own. We learn from observing the performance of other people or groups—both those we see as our superiors and those we see as our inferiors. And we observe the wins and losses of those we think are most like us. From these observations we set our levels of aspiration.

Of course, we understand that going for a higher-than-realistic achievement level may require risky or desperate strategies that ultimately lead to our losing everything. While rounding the mark and into the next leg in a sailing race, we may decide to stay with the fleet knowing we can end up in the middle. But there is also the risky option of leaving the fleet and looking for the wind or the tide that, if found, would bring victory—but that, if not found, would assure us of last place. So it is with stock investments. Do we go for the big risk, hoping for a big win but possibly getting wiped out? Or for the safe investment with minimum yield? Or do we invest for a middle-range return?

There are obvious individual differences in the willingness to take risk, but studies have not been able to find any personality traits consistently related to such differences in risk-taking behavior. Some people set their aspirations so high that they often fail. Others set lower levels and more often exceed their aspirations. In raising aspirations after winning, one person may advance slowly, inch by inch or 5 percent at a time, while another attempts 50-percent increases in achievement. Even though social research confirms that these differences exist, they have been hard to explain.

Social custom influences us to set our aspirations higher. In our daily lives, the mass media intrude to influence our standards. The rising aspirations for good health have exceeded what is realistic. As a result, since about 1970, health professionals in both England and the United States are encountering more self-reported ailments than before, when the definition of "feeling well" was set at a lower level. Similarly, "how to" books on sexual fulfillment may have raised performance expectations and thus increased a sense of inadequacy.

Some parents pressure their young children to be high achievers starting at age two in their first days in preschool. Because of parental pressure, some of our brightest high school pupils are led to cheat to raise their grades and get into college. The parents want to raise the level of achievement from one generation to the next; if they went to the University of Miami, they may want their children to go to the University of Michigan. Most of the children do not get into the college of their choice because they are aiming too high, setting sights on the top ten colleges only.

Sometimes we are called upon to try to win when even the best of us would expect to lose; the level of expected achievement is set too high for us. In sports, this situation is familiar. In school, even when we are unprepared for examinations because we did not study, we must take the test, knowing we will fail. In military patrols, raids, or invasions, although the chances of success are slim and the chances of dying high, we go.

Occasionally we are counseled to lower our aspirations. In the introduction to *Robinson Crusoe*, Daniel Defoe wrote about how, when he wished to leave home to seek his fortune, his father tried to persuade him to stay:

> He called me one morning into his chamber. . . . He asked me what reasons . . . I had for leaving my father's house and my native country, where I . . . had a prospect of raising my fortunes by application and industry, with a life of ease and pleasure. He told me it was for men of desperate fortunes on one hand, or of aspiring, superior fortunes on the other, who went abroad upon adven-

tures, to rise by enterprise, and make themselves famous . . . that these things were all either too far above me, or too far below me; that mine was the middle state, or what might be called the upper station of low life, which he had found by long experience was the best state in the world.

Proverbs support all three levels of aspiration. In England and the United States, we are familiar with Browning's "Ah, but a man's reach should exceed his grasp,/Or what's a heaven for?" But a Yiddish proverb says, "He that lies on the ground cannot fall." Somewhere between these two, the Taoists say, "Live below your capacity"; and Confucius and the ancient Greeks urge upon us a life of balance, moderation, and the "golden mean."

THE VALUE OF SECOND PLACE

If we keep in mind the subjective nature of personal aspirations, then we will understand cases of the "sore winner." Others may say a person has won, but the winner waves off compliments for the achievement and is disdainful of the win because of the not too well hidden belief that he or she is better than the actual achievement—like Rick Carey, the twenty-year-old swimmer in the 1984 Olympics who won the gold medal in the 200-meter backstroke but was angry because he expected to set a new world record.

Scientists whose work receives a lot of media coverage sometimes are angry at the news reports because they believe they have done or can do much better work than what is being publicized. Harriet Zuckerman, the sociologist who has studied Nobel Prize winners in the United States, summarizes what these extraordinary achievers said when asked about their scientific work for which they received the prize: "Nearly half of the laureates who were interviewed, while conceding the scientific significance of their research, were convinced that it was not their best work."

We also understand the "happy loser." Placing second in a contest may not be considered a loss if our performance exceeds our expectations. If we know ahead of time that winning is not possible, then our aspiration may become simply to make our best effort and make it close. Subjectively, this is winning. I hear "second place only pays off at the racetrack," but this is not always true. Whether it pays off depends on what we are after. If we are shooting for first place and miss it, then there is no pay-off. If we are shooting for third place and win second, then our victory is even greater than we hoped.

In the 1976 film *Rocky,* for example, the world heavyweight champion plans a fight in Philadelphia. It is not a title fight but an exhibition, and the promoter must set up a match with a local fighter. Rocky, who is asked to fight the champion, experiences a process of setting and changing aspirations somewhat as follows: He starts out saying, "I thought I would be his sparring partner in town." "He's the best, I'm a ham and egger; wouldn't be much of a fight," and then, "Just do the best I can." He finds a mentor, a seventy-six-year-old trainer. He goes into training (some of the most famous scenes of the film). The night before the fight, he thinks, "I can't beat him. The Las Vegas odds are I won't last three rounds." And then: "No matter if I lose this fight, all I want to do is go the distance. Nobody has ever gone the distance . . . then I'll know I'm not just another bum from the neighborhood." In the fight he does go the distance, even fights better toward the end. He loses the fight—but, as Montaigne said, "There are defeats more triumphant than victories."

"Who invented second place?" we can ask. Who thought of different sizes of reward according to first, second, and third place? In describing the first thousand years of the Olympics, M. I. Finley and H. W. Pleket write, "Always to be first and to surpass the others must be understood literally and strictly." There was no second place or third place, no silver or bronze medal. "Victory alone brought glory—defeat brought undying shame." Competitors aspired to "either the wreath or death."

In Rome, the first recorded combat of gladiators was 264 B.C. This event reached its peak there in the period A.D. 50 to 100. Gladiators sometimes fought wild beasts, but mainly they fought each other. They fought one against one, with no handicapping and almost no element of luck—just pure effort, winner takes all, and no second chance for the dead loser.

At some time during the evolution of the Olympics, the "winner takes all" competition changed to make room for second- and third-place contestants. This subject has not been studied historically, and the origin of the concept of second and third place in different cultures, in periods in history, and organizations, is not well known. Those who have thought about it believe that something peculiar to English culture produced this concept. In the legends of Robin Hood, which date from about A.D. 1100, the archery contests always had three prizes. Perhaps the custom had its beginnings in horse racing, but why, and why three prizes?

In all societies around the world, there are some situations in which only one person prospers, and other situations in which the rules specify sharing in some form or other. In general, there are two lines of thought about why the "winner takes all" event evolved into situations where success is shared. Both of these explanations are probably true; they do not contradict each other.

The first comes from analyses of economic behavior and of betting in sports and in games. In game theory, we talk of a "zero sum game" in which what one player wins, another must lose. But there are also "non-zero sum" games where the amounts to be won are spread among many players and everybody can win, usually different amounts. Indeed, theoretically it is even possible that all can be equal in what they win. Game theory describes the conditions under which, on average, the strategy of sharing a prize will produce more gains for the competitors than if one winner were to take all. The reward will be smaller, but so will be the risk of losing and getting nothing at all. Presumably through human history, the social rules have evolved to define those events in our daily lives where the best strategy for all was to share the prize.

The second explanation holds that the progress of civilization has brought with it a democratization of success. Thus, different grades of winning were introduced so that more people win at least something. This change may have come from a recognition that in order to keep society intact and cohesive, to keep people in the contest, there needed to be more than one big winner, with everyone else losing. A socially recognized and honored ranking of achievement levels adds external recognition and reward to our subjective satisfaction in having come that far.

MANAGING THE BIG WIN

Although changing levels of aspiration is, like changing time-tables, an easy method to use, in dealing with winning it some-times fails us. One of the challenges produced by winning is to reset aspirations, raising them to a higher level of difficulty. Usually this is easy to do: our aspirations float with the situation. I have heard that a man said about his private jet ($650,000 to buy and $300,000 to operate), "When I bought it, it was a luxu-ry. Two weeks later it was a necessity." He was living proof of the principle put forth by the manager of one of the world's great hotels: "People, I find, are very easily spoiled—whatever you give them they start to demand." Then there is the cartoon of a man sitting at his desk, in gold cuff links and a dark suit with wide chalk stripes; there are on his desk three telephones, and on his wall the framed motto: "MORE."

Sometimes we have definite ideas about what we would do after winning: new friends we would make, things we would buy, places we would live, what we would work on next. For some of us, though, the time comes in life when we are hit with a big win that exceeds even our ideal level of aspiration. We win too much—success beyond our wildest dreams. I think that in antici-pation of losing we make alternate plans, but in anticipation of winning we only imagine our rewards and do not plan beyond that moment of success. We are not ready. We are unprepared for victory. Rising to a new level is not easy. It is not always true that (as I believe Nelson Doubleday, owner of the Mets, said) "all problems disappear when you're a winner." And this comment is attributed to one of our foremost American actors who said, "I always thought the losers became alcoholic; I didn't know the winners did, too."

We do try to keep our aspirations in tune with reality. A few years ago a 310-pound defensive tackle who plays for the Chicago Bears suddenly became a national celebrity. William ("The Refrigerator") Perry in a four-week period ran the ball for yardage, caught a pass for a touchdown, and ran for another. It was the first time a defensive tackle had ever, in the history of football, been given the ball to carry to make a touchdown. The American public was captivated by this out-of-the-ordinary event—which was said to put the fun back in football. Perry became a television star, appearing on the "Tonight" show, the "Today" show, and the nightly network news shows. There were requests (perhaps one hundred per day) for endorsements, and $750,000 and more in fees came his way. Meanwhile his mother said, "I know he was good, but I don't think he's that good." His wife said, "This was great for a while, but now it's ridiculous. It's gotten out of hand." Perry himself said, "As fast as it comes, that's how fast it goes." He was right. Now it is as if the event had never happened.

There are aberrations in how we shift our aspirations after winning. Psychologists writing about the pathological gambler have found that one invariably has a history of a big win:

> The big win establishes in the mind of the gambler that it could happen again, and could be even larger. . . . An attitude of unreasonable optimism about winning begins to become a classical part of gamblers' style. . . . The amount of money gamblers bet escalates because they anticipate still-larger wins. Then, they encounter a losing streak that is difficult to tolerate. . . . They gamble with sources of money they have earned, saved, or invested in order to get even. . . . They must get their money back, and they begin to "chase.". . . At this point, gamblers are borrowing heavily.

In the reverse case, one may try to make no change at all, but I do not think we can act as if success had not occurred without our paying some price. The author Lawrence Sanders became rich and famous in midlife. After twenty-five years of writing with a simple income, he now has sold many millions of his books. He says, though:

I lead a dull life. . . . If my financial success had come at age 25 instead of 50, I'd have bought yachts, everything would be different. But my style of living hasn't changed all that much. I don't travel, except to my place in New York twice a year. I drink the same vodka, the same cognac I did before. I don't have any hobbies. I read—and I write.

He describes his life as lonely and miserable.

One Christmas two young boys were sitting, opening presents, on the floor around the Christmas tree. The older boy, whose aspiration level was higher and seemed almost limitless, was looking for one more present after another, raising his aspiration level as rapidly as the presents came. The younger boy, in contrast, was pounding on the floor, saying, "No more presents," wanting instead to play with the three or four he had already, which already exceeded his ideal aspiration.

More complex was the experience of the actor LaVar Burton, who starred in the TV hit "Roots," in the role of the young slave Kunta Kinte. Suddenly almost everyone in the United States knew Burton's face:

"It was . . . something," Burton said. . . . "I've watched people have car accidents over seeing me on the street. Imagine what that feels like. . . .

"I was confused about everything. Where I was going, everything. People told me my whole life was going to change, and they were right. One day I looked up and I was really confused, I was really hurt. . . . It hurt. I was in bad trouble, and I didn't know what was going on."

Lottery winners are pure cases of the "big win" and of the burden of winning. Winning a lottery is not the same as succeeding in love or work. It is a general, across-the-board extraordinary gain in capacity, that allows you to exceed your dreams in many sectors of life all at once. Suddenly you have the means to achieve almost all of your goals that money can buy, and do it right now. Many of the current challenges in your life are swept away by this torrent of wealth. Now the task is to create the new challenges.

The German film director Erich Von Stroheim, in his 1924 classic *Greed*, portrays the disintegration of a woman's character that follows after she wins a $5,000 lottery. In contrast, most contemporary books, films, or television shows about lottery winners in the United States portray them as elated, joyous, liberated, living happily ever after.

Research shows that Von Stroheim had the truth. A study of lottery winners, comparing them with people not involved in lotteries, shows that the winners are not happier than the others now, nor do they expect to be in the future. In fact, the winners rated seven ordinary activities as less enjoyable now—such as talking with a friend, eating breakfast, getting a compliment, reading a magazine, or buying clothes. A new life has to be created. One lottery player says, "If I can just get over the hump . . . ," but it just leads to another, and bigger, hump straight ahead. A wise friend called me on the day after the drawing for the $60,000,000 Florida lottery and said, "Did you hear the good news? My wife didn't win the lottery."

Most winners do make material improvements in life style, including quitting their job, buying a new car or new home, taking care of medical problems (both their own and those of relatives), and setting aside money to put children and grandchildren through college. A lottery winner in Turkey, a blue-collar worker, said to his friends, "Now I only eat the center of the onion" (onion sandwiches being the usual lunch diet of the Turkish working class).

The problems begin as these winners restructure their lives, trying to establish the new level of just manageable difficulty. A doughnut maker at Dunkin' Donuts quit his job when he won, bought new furniture and a jeep; but when he feels bored and depressed, he goes back to work for a few days: "It was much easier when I was just a simple baker."

A woman who won $5 million in a Canadian lottery bought a house to be near her son, on whom her family said she doted. News reports at the time said that she had once tipped a man $7,000 just to play pool with her son. She was trying to break up her son's marriage, and now, with her new resources, negotiated a contract for $5,000 to kill his twenty-three-year-old wife. She was found out and charged with soliciting first-degree murder.

A scholar who has been studying lottery winners for many years concludes, "They won the battle against poverty and deprivation, but are losing the war; they are financial successes, but social and psychological casualties."

SCALING DOWN THE DREAM

Our aspirations sink with our failures as we lower the level of difficulty to a point we can manage. For instance, romantic love is a powerfully motivating goal for human beings. Although many people stop short of using words like *ambition* or *winning and losing* in intimate areas of life—we seem to need to believe that somewhere in life there are good and gentle places where winning and losing events never occur—the fact is that winning and losing in love is the theme of many popular operas, plays, books, and so on. People in psychotherapy often express the wish to be close to another person—in the family or in a romance—and say they want this more than anything in the world. Men and women in their thirties, searching for love, may be unmarried because they have been unable to find their dream mate. They have been through a long and active search, including perhaps several tryouts that did not work. There may be a brief return to new and improbable behavior—going to dangerous singles' bars, responding to sleazy advertisements for finding a mate—the last-chance syndrome again. The level of aspiration is still high and the timetable stretched out, but the clock is ticking. In the end, they will have to settle for less.

Wealthy investors, stung by the stock market crash in 1987, had to change their plans. No longer just stretching timetables, they now write off their highest hopes. One gives up the idea of enough money to establish a dynasty, and tries to accept the $3-million level, thinking how little each of his children would inherit. Another shifts from thinking about hitting the $1-million mark to keeping what she has and trying to match inflation with modest growth. Middle-income investors now aim to make a few thousand dollars to augment their income. Young investment bankers thought it was great while it lasted, but now are willing to settle for a few crumbs.

The main body of research on shrinking aspirations is about work careers. For most timed and ordered careers, positions can be ranked according to money, power, and prestige. The nearer you get to the top, the harder it is to move up the pyramid. In general, at each step up the corporate ladder, there are 30 percent fewer jobs than on the rung below. Young lawyers joining a firm may work sixty-hour weeks for six or seven years and then only one fourth of them become partners. Out of the one thousand who work in an advertising firm, at least one hundred, if not more, may mistakenly believe they will end up with the top job.

As children we are taught to have high career aspirations, and then we confront the reality of the workplace. Every day, I suppose, thousands of us are dealing with the new realization that our youthful dreams of career achievement will not come true. It is remarkable how easy this restructuring seems to be. In California, for instance, a long-term study that has followed people from childhood through adulthood reports that more than half of forty-year-olds still aspire to advance, but less than one fifth of the fifty-year-olds want to move up; and this change has occurred without any signs of crisis.

In his research, Robert Faulkner shows the downward shift in aspirations for the two occupations he studied intensively: hockey players and orchestra musicians. The expectations for achieving a top-level position while still in the "minor leagues" dropped from 53 percent to 43 percent as the hockey players passed the age of twenty-four. For the orchestra musicians, as they aged from their early twenty's to middle thirty's the drop was from 72 percent to 22 percent. Faulkner adds, "This kind of personal adaptation is rarely consummated in one dramatic moment or turning point. Rather it is contained in a process of self-redefinition that extends over a period of time."

In a study of young executives at AT&T during the first years of their careers, Douglas Bray and his colleagues report:

> One of the clearest personal changes in this group of young recruits was a rapid and decisive move in the direction of greater

realism concerning the job. At the outset of the study most of the subjects were assuming that the organization they were entering was a veritable utopia. All bosses would be inspiring leaders, ability was to be quickly recognized and rewarded, peers would be stimulating, and a vice presidency was doubtless lurking somewhere in the future, ready to pounce when the time was ripe.

This unblushing optimism faded rapidly. . . . In a few years the fourth level of management rather than the sixth or seventh typified an ambitious goal for the average man.

Some aspirations are of little importance to us, and we can reduce them with ease. Others mean more to us, and we may never get over our failure to fulfill them. Psychiatrists may say that giving up part of our lives should cause mourning over the loss. This may indeed happen during the transition, and may last longer than that in some cases. But the more likely emotion is joy at finally ridding ourselves of hopes that have turned heavy with disappointment. In the end it is relief, not grief, we feel as we relax into a state of lowered ambition.

10

Changing Goals

In the beginning of this book, I described a bit of the variety in our goals and then two of the ways in which these goals can be categorized: competitive or cooperative; selfish or altruistic. Three other characteristics make it harder or easier to change goals following success or failure. These are: whether we have few or many goals; how they are clustered into families; and how they are linked together in a sequence of achievements.

DEPTH OR BREADTH

Each of us who is fortunate enough in life to have a choice may try for one truly extraordinary achievement or to do several things well. In most societies, the prizes go to the unusual achievements. We value those people who devote their lives toward one goal, who live with one main purpose which in the end they accomplish. People with more modest achievements spread over many areas receive less acclaim.

The psychologist Anders Ericsson and his colleagues have studied world-class achievers among pianists, musical composers, and chess players. Their research gives us an insight into what is required to achieve excellence in a single domain. It is not inborn genius that produces exceptional success; rather, it is sustained, intense training from an early age. Pianists began at age six; composers, ages six to nine; chess players, about age nine. Attaining an international level of performance after these early starts still required seventeen years for pianists and over fourteen years for chess players. The age of peak performance was between thirty and forty years for composers and chess players.

Sometimes a price must be paid for this intensity. Consider an unusual mathematical genius, Srinigar Ramanujan, a poor, uneducated but Brahman Indian born a century ago.

> In 1909, when he was 22, he married a nine-year-old and took a clerical position to support her and her mother. . . . While he worked as a clerk he continued to pour out math results, using excess wrapping from the office to scribble down his formulas. He was so obsessed with his mathematics that he did not want to stop even to eat and his wife would feed him at mealtime so that he would be free to continue writing while he ate. He was discovered and brought to England but life was not so easy for him there. He left his wife behind and had no one with him to be sure he ate or slept. Because he cared more for mathematics than eating or sleeping . . . he would work for long stretches, 24 to 36 hours[,] . . . then would collapse and sleep for 12 hours or more. . . . In 1917 he came down with a mysterious illness that may have been Vitamin B12 deficiency caused by his poor diet.

Weak and incapacitated, he returned in 1919 to India and died a year later.

To have one goal of overriding value may be like Macbeth's ambition for the crown of Scotland—an obsession close to madness. The *South China Morning Post*, reported on a "madman of the forest" who had been honored by the government of the People's Republic of China. In 1966, at the age of sixty-six, he abandoned his life as a clothing merchant, left his wife of more than forty years and the rest of his family, to live in a mountain cave and plant trees: "'He lived on yams and wild herbs with a little bean, corn and millet,' a report said. 'For more than 10 years he did not buy himself new clothes or new shoes.'" Working alone with a hoe, "'Zhang Houla, now 83, has planted more than one million trees in a remote valley and hill slope'" in north-central China.

It is a risky business to spend all of one's life in pursuit of a single goal, developing no other interests along the way or leaving them behind, burning bridges behind you. The narrowly committed identity is vulnerable. The danger is that if the game is lost, it is difficult to change goals.

A few of us go to the other extreme. We try to be the kind of person who has "done everything, some of them twice"; or as one woman said about another, "No matter what I bring up, she has either done it or she's been there." A poet writes:

> *I am greedy, Puritans scold me*
> *for running breathlessly*
> *over life's table of contents*
> *and for wishing and longing for everything.*

Most of us walk a middle path between being spread too thin and having a single-minded commitment to one goal over a long period of time. A widely used personality test covering more than twenty areas of interest (such as social activities, writing, adventure, agriculture, nature), yields a profile of an individual showing the areas of most and least interest. Some people have a flat profile; they are in the average range of interest in almost all the areas. Others show intense concentration in one area of interest and low interest scores in the other twenty or so. Between these extremes of breadth and depth are most of us, with a high interest in five or six areas and less concern with the others.

There is value in having a number of goals in life when dealing with winning and losing. The two most fundamental sectors of life, those of work and family, illustrate how we can balance out our successes and failures. Studies of the prestige ranking we give to occupations find that those of garbage collector (now "sanitation worker"), bartender, street sweeper, and shoe shiner have the lowest standing. All parts of the population, including those who actually hold these jobs, agree on these rankings. Nonetheless, bartenders and garbage collectors have high self-respect. The reason: several national studies in the United States show that workers in these low-status occupations focused mainly on their families as their area of achievement. Of all the occupations, garbage collectors ranked lowest in occupational repute and in their self-esteem about their line of work, but were second highest in their pride in their families. Mail carriers were the highest, and bartenders ranked third. College professors, who are near the top in occupational prestige, are low in their pride and self-esteem about their families.

If I take the middle path, though, I will die curious about two things. On the one side are all those experiences I never got around to trying: classical music, carpentry, singing, acting, photography, painting, politics, power, social service, hang-gliding, chess, mountain climbing, dog sledding, spending a year in the desert. On the other side may have been that single majestic achievement I could have created if my life had been completely devoted to the solitary purpose. W. H. Auden writes:

> *O plunge your hands in water;*
> *plunge them in up to the wrist.*
> *Stare, stare in the basin*
> *and wonder what you've missed.*

FAMILIES OF GOALS

A sculptor starting to work on a given morning looks around the barn studio and decides which sculpture to work on during that day. A lawyer thinks about the many current clients as sheep wandering about the meadows and plans how to bring them safely home. An author muses about four or five partially completed writing projects and wonders how to get them finished. For most of us, the goals we seek are organized into these clusters or "families" of subgoals. Within a work career, there may be a half-dozen specific interests that can be worked on and moved ahead.

Among our financial concerns, we can be trying to raise our income, reduce our debt, increase our savings. In regard to health, we think about improving diet, losing weight, getting rid of addictions, exercising (with even more choices here, for example, among swimming, walking, or exercising with equipment).

In rare instances, we concentrate 100 percent on a particular goal—say, when we are in the middle of a tough squash match we very much want to win. Sometimes our concentration is more like 5 percent, if we are listening to an aimless group discussion, while thinking about many other things. Usually we are engaged on multiple fronts at the same time. How do we keep track of all this?

Imagine that you have a large monitor screen the size of a living room wall to show your goals in life at a point in time. The screen would display perhaps eight or ten sectors of life activity—children, spouse or companion, work, money, health, friendship, religion—and within each would show the cluster of specific goals related to the different children, the different components of your finances, your health interests. Each of these would have three indicator lights of different colors. A flashing red light would mean you have just suffered a loss related to that sector; green would signify a big win; and amber, a steady state for this time. There might be thirty or forty of these triads of indicator lights, constantly changing colors, all across the screen.

You would be in different phases of reorganizing your life in the different sectors, all at the same time. Some of this is easy; some, hard. In one sector, you are raising your sights or speeding up or finding new goals; but in others, you are lowering your aspirations, or postponing your achievements to even farther in the future, or struggling with giving up a goal forever.

You do not deal with these wins and losses hour by hour. You cannot constantly check each area of interest—like continually taking your pulse—computing new levels of just manageable difficulty, and making new plans accordingly. You do not program your life by such close monitoring. Rather, the experience accumulates in your mind, staying at the preconscious level (unless it is a major win or loss, a big event). Then there comes a day when you take stock—a New Year's Eve, a birthday, a vacation—

when you sum up your life to see how you are doing. You can look across your various fields of action and conclude, "Not bad," or, "I'm losing ground." If you are generally doing well, you make this summation rapidly. You do not often sit down and write out all the good things that have happened.

Losses or anxieties about possible losses are different. A string of setbacks may suggest that a general retreat is in order. Awareness of these occurring across the wide screen of activity will accumulate in the preconscious. But there comes a time when one has to sit down to figure out what is going wrong—a dumped-out worry list that clears the mind.

When these events require us to reset our ambitions, it is easier to change subgoals than to shift into and out of a main area of life. Mothers and fathers can give up their aspirations for one of their children who has a deviant life style that they cannot accept. But to give up on all one's children is very different. We can hardly replace our love and concern for all of our children, if they all turn out badly, by deciding that we are going to try to get rich instead. Exiting from or adding another of these major families of goals is a major reformation of life, involving new social groups as points of reference and fundamental changes in our self-image.

THE EMPTINESS OF SUCCESS

How long can we enjoy a win and savor victory? One of the truths of our human condition is that we rest and are satisfied for a minute, an hour, a day, perhaps a year, and then feel we must move on.

No doubt there are individual differences in how long our feelings last. Some people move on to the next event even before consummation, a Don Juan on the verge of an orgasm already thinking about the next conquest. Others strive to hold onto the feeling, to stretch it out. In the end, as I have said, our drive for growth and mastery propels us from a winning episode to setting a new and more difficult task. The substance of the achievement—in work, family, health, wealth, whatever sector of life—

does not make much difference in how long we feel happy. Even the elation or despair coming from the biggest events in our lives lasts only a bit longer than the ordinary.

Most winning episodes are rewarding because we usually are correct in our appraisal of what our goals are and what they will bring. We are happy with our effort and happy with the achievement. There are occasions, though, when we do not feel the happiness we expected. I see three reasons why this may occur.

First, the amount of time and effort required to achieve a given goal may be so great that it causes failure in other important areas of life. Life becomes unbalanced. Nothing is left to use outside of the activity consuming us.

Usually we think about unbalanced lives in terms of work careers, but the same could be said about excessive demands of the parental role. When a parent has several small, close-in-age children, their care may squeeze out other domains of life, leading to loss of interest in the spouse, underachievement in a career, and decline in physical health. Or, we try to set up a health regimen and establish control over our health, only to find that it takes so much time and effort that the rest of our life goes out of control. We end up poisoning with one hand while creating with the other.

Sometimes when we overinvest in one domain of our lives, we open our eyes to what it has cost us only after the goal has been reached. An author friend writes:

> When one of my books arrived in the mail, the few minutes of flushed satisfaction were quickly followed by realization of how neglected and lonely my youngest daughter had been during the previous 18 months of my working on it. I cried. My husband had to prevent my throwing the book into the fireplace! After another "win" [her fourth book], I realized how awful our housekeeper was. She should have been fired months earlier, but that fragile Rube Goldberg domestic apparatus was too important to the work in progress to bear close inspection. The painful price of the process of blissful absorption in one domain for neglect/loneliness/poor performance in another domain had to be paid.

A second reason is described as "fear of falling." When the success is seen as the result of luck or other external causes rather than one's own effort, problems may arise. If we believe that our own actions brought success, we can be happy, proud, full of gratitude or even relief upon winning; but if we believe our success was undeserved, then we are embarrassed, or guilt-ridden, or feel like an imposter who will be discovered and exposed.

A friend told me, "I'm interested in how individuals deal with discrepancies between achievements and aspirations in which the former exceed the latter. I'm not so sure that for some individuals this is as easy to cope with as one might think. For example, when I was in a sort of modified psychoanalysis, I used to tell my analyst that . . . people were going to discover that I was not especially bright; that one day I was going to be 'caught' and exposed as a fake; and so on. Now, I certainly didn't feel as bad as I might have had I been thinking that I had not achieved anything close to what I had aspired to, but I nevertheless felt troubled. She responded that nearly every successful person she knew felt this way and that it was a pretty common phenomenon."

Steven Berglas, a psychologist who specializes in studying success-induced disorders, gives some examples. The astronaut Buzz Aldrin, for instance, on his second "man-on-the-moon" walk, found himself in a position where something immense happened to him—"an almost lethal dose of non-contingent success." He cannot follow it up by raising the level of aspiration or turning to a different set of goals. There seems to be no place to go but down. In another case (where the process of self-handicapping I described earlier appears), Berglas describes the hockey player Derek Sanderson, who was a few years ago the highest-paid athlete on earth. "The problem," writes Berglas, "was that Sanderson couldn't figure out what he'd done to deserve such status. He was fearful he couldn't perform as expected. He began drinking, so that after attaining initial success . . . he can attribute his subsequent failure to alcohol, not lack of ability."

A third reason why winning may not bring happiness is we may be wrong about the value of the goal. We thought it would be one thing, and it turns out to be something else. I think of Sidney Greenstreet's face when he scrapes the paint off the Maltese Falcon and sees that it is made of lead, not gold. One may dream for a long time about marrying a particular person or about traveling to one of the world's great cities. Then, when the dream is fulfilled, the person or the city may not be what was expected. One may seek a major career promotion, achieve it, and then, after waiting for two or three years, realize it is not what one expected. In a *Life* magazine interview of Barbara Walters, the author Chris Chase observes, "But somehow she doesn't believe it all. 'If I am so important,' she says, 'why doesn't something happen?'"

REACHING THE TOP

We can think of our goals as a series of ladders, stretching upward. We climb one ladder to the top, reach a platform, and then there is another ladder to climb. Our goals are linked vertically in means-to-ends relationships. Thus, Murphy's Sixth Corollary says, "Whenever you set out to do something, something else must be done first."

The goals we look for as steps to something more are called "instrumental goals." Most often they serve several purposes. To a teenager, getting a driver's license leads to other goals—independence from parents, dating, travel, prestige within a peer group. To the alcoholic, giving up drinking is the means to many other ends: better health, self-respect, responsibility on the job, family acceptance, regained love.

Usually we recognize that the goal we are working toward, however much we may value it in itself, is still just a step toward reaching something else we have in mind. At other times, we believe that the goal is the final end, and that if we achieve it we will have no more to do in this line of endeavor. But in most of human life there are no final ends, no terminal goals. The achievement of what we thought was our final purpose only opens up more that can be done; and in hindsight, the end we pursued turns out to be instrumental to new ends. The ladders we climb do not go anywhere, except to more ladders. We do not stop when we are winning.

Fame, creativity, wealth, doing good, and other long-term life goals usually are so abstract that there is no specific level of achievement at which we can say we have reached the end. I knew one twenty-year-old woman who had the open-ended goal of creating beauty in all parts of life, with the subgoals of creating physical beauty in homes and gardens, beauty in the fine arts, and beauty in interpersonal relationships. A young man wrote in his notebook over and over, "I will be rich"—and so he became during his life, continually raising his sights after achieving one level after another. Another woman recalls how from high school on she always wanted to be at the top: "It didn't really matter where I ended up. . . . All I cared about . . . was that I be successful at whatever it was." Now in midlife, she tells her friends that within five years she "hopes—and fully intends—to land a cabinet post, an executive position in a major corporation, or a spot as a television talk-show host." Another middle-aged person, a man, said to me, "It must be nice to have something you can do until you die."

For a few people, success is so complete—their highest goals have been reached—that there seems to be nowhere to go. One man in his early forties won the top administrative position in his profession, and people said to him, "What will you go on to next?"—expressing an image of the ladder that still had more rungs to climb; but others said, "What can you find to do after this?"—expressing a climax image, that there was nothing more than this line of achievement.

Tenzing Norgay, the Sherpa guide with Edmund Hillary in 1953, said after completing the successful climb of Mt. Everest, "I am a lucky man. I have had a dream and it has come true, and that is not a thing that happens often to men." What did he do when there was no higher mountain to climb? What happens to people who have become among the best in the world in some field? William Faulkner mused about what would happen to writers in this situation:

> All of us failed to match our dream of perfection. So I rate us on the basis of our splendid failure to do the impossible. In my opinion, if I could write all my work again, I am convinced that I would do it better, which is the healthiest condition for an artist.

That's why he keeps on working, trying again; he believes each time that this time he will do it, bring it off. Of course he won't, which is why this condition is healthy. Once he did it, once he matched the work to the image, the dream, nothing would remain but to cut his throat, jump off the other side of that pinnacle of perfection into suicide.

Those who are fortunate will find another mountain. Generals of the army and air force moved to presidencies in major universities during the 1960s: this is not mountain climbing, this is only pinnacle hopping. Dwight Eisenhower made another move, to become President of the United States (1952). Linus Pauling, with his Nobel Prize in chemistry (1954), won a second for peace (1962). During the Vietnam War, Benjamin Spock became a pacifist leader in addition to being the country's most famous pediatrician. Jane Fonda became a political activist as well as an actress. Benny Goodman added classical music to his jazz achievements. Astronauts, after their trips through space, have gone into politics, searched for Noah's Ark, and turned inward with personal religious striving to change themselves.

For some it is hard to find the way. A friend in his late thirties, unmarried, a loner, forged an unusual life style. He would say, "I am always rebuilding my life out of the ashes of my success." He was a person of exceptional ability who would rise rapidly toward the top of whatever line of work he went into. Evidently he was unable, though, to find ways to keep on raising the challenges in his life so that he would find it interesting. Instead, as he became more and more successful in a line of endeavor, he would quit completely. After perhaps a year of alcoholism and living on the street, he would pull himself together and start over again at the bottom, in another line of work. An extreme case, to be sure, but he understood that there are no achievements that have lasting satisfaction. We must find new things to work on, set our sights higher, work harder and faster when we have won. We cannot sit around and wait for something good to happen.

The despair of the poet Allen Ginsberg is described by the critic Helen Vendler: "Everything is already known, and everything has stopped happening. . . . Friends are now what they will be for good: no one would change. Everything has been encountered: sex, love, friendship, drugs, even fame, even the boundary dimensions of self."

Some of the great never make the move at all and are, in the end, victims of their own success. A year or two before the painter Jackson Pollock's death (1956), his neighbor "asked Pollock how it felt to have made it. . . . The answer came back: 'Lousy. . . . When you've done it, turns out you're done for—in yourself you're nowhere and no one. . . . You're caught, only nothing's holding you. . . . You got to go somewhere, to the edge of something, but there's no edge.'"

LETTING GO

Finding new goals after winning is one thing; giving up a goal after failing is another. The end of the line has come, and nothing has worked. We have to acknowledge the failure and take the hit.

Whether a goal is hard or easy to relinquish, some of us are always slow to change. We continue to try to retrieve what the economists call "sunk costs," and often put good money after bad in our lives. We have failed to learn to cut our losses.

We try to carry everything along, giving up nothing, as in Robert Frost's "The Armful":

> For every parcel I stoop down to seize,
> I lose some other off my arms and knees,
> And the whole pile is slipping, bottles, buns,
> Extremes too hard to comprehend at once,
> Yet nothing I should care to leave behind.
> With all I have to hold with, hand and mind
> And heart, if need be, I will do my best
> To keep their building balanced at my breast.
> I crouch down to prevent them as they fall;
> Then sit down in the middle of them all.
> I had to drop the armful in the road
> And try to stack them in a better load.

There are times when we conclude that something we hope for may never happen, no matter how much time we give it, and that we must face it and stop trying to delay the inevitable. Still, sometimes we persist, our ambition fading into fantasy, and miraculously things work out. Frank B. Bourgin, now seventy-seven years old and physically disabled, was a graduate student in political science at the University of Chicago forty years ago.

> For more than four decades, his Ph.D. dissertation remained locked in a steel box, the bitter legacy of an academic future that had died when a faculty committee at the University of Chicago rejected the manuscript.
> But Frank P. Bourgin's dream of someday receiving his Ph.D. in political science did not die. It haunted him, as he raised a family and made his living in business and in the Federal bureaucracy.

He made another effort to get his dissertation accepted by sending a summary to Arthur Schlesinger, Jr., the historian, who urged Chicago's political science department to take a second look:

> And now, in an unlikely ending to years of frustration, Mr. Bourgin is about to be recognized as a scholar who was ahead of his time. After taking a new look at the 45-year-old dissertation, the political science faculty decided that the department had erred when it rejected the paper. Later this spring, the university will award Mr. Bourgin his Ph.D.

For most of us, however, fantasies like this one do not come true. We see that the odds are increasingly stacked against winning. The future's great promise is fading.

Others of us, in contrast, are quick to give up a losing endeavor. We might agree with this personality test statement: "I could cut my moorings, . . . quit my home, my family, and my friends . . . . without suffering great regrets." People who seem lucky may be that way because they are quick to realize they are losing, cut their losses, give up a goal, and start up something else that they are more likely to win.

I believe that in general individuals let most goals pass away with scarcely a sense of loss. Some women insist that the issue of "fading beauty" involves a real sense of loss (one not shared by men), but other women think of it as a passage into an age when they can just be themselves and no longer need to strive to be attractive. Men may work at being lean and muscular, but eventually it is beyond their control and they give up, too. An overweight man at a cocktail party was struggling to maintain a fit body image by pulling his belt tight across the middle of his ample stomach, but he had to keep hitching the belt up and holding it in place. Uncomfortable and unhappy, finally he undid the belt, wrapped it under his belly—"down and under"—pulled it tight, and, with a sense of relief, gave up that goal forever.

Some goals are harder to let go. A thirty-five-year-old woman said that she and her husband would buy a house, but later in their lives than their parents had. The couple have no money and need to save enough for the down payment. Four years later, she said that they actually see themselves as losing ground, not gaining bit by bit against the future or even holding steady. They see now that they will never own a home.

An older man, a friend of mine, had a youthful dream of living for a month on each of the world's twenty greatest beaches—white, pink, red, gold, black. Soon he was working, married with a family, and spending two years of his life on this journey was impossible. As time went on, the dream got smaller. A half-year trip to the ten best beaches still was possible—heading east around the world through southwest Mexico, Costa Rica, Grenada, the Seychelles, the Maldives, Java, Palau, Kuaii. In later life, it seemed that just a month in Bora Bora would be achievable, but it never happened. Instead, he became an armchair traveler, viewing whatever videotapes and travelogues about beaches were available. In the end, he never got to any of the beaches.

Like our aspirations, it seems to be easier to let go of goals when we have lost than to find new purposes after we have succeeded. We leave much of our past behind us. It becomes dim in our memory; and when we revisit our past, many of the early dreams seem unfamiliar, as if they belonged to a stranger. It is as if we came across a bunch of unmarked keys that have accumulated over the years, and think, "Where did they fit? What did they unlock? Could I still use them?" But we do not know, and we move on.

THE ELUSIVE MIDLIFE CRISIS

Similar to the myths about gender, culture, and ambition discussed in chapter 1 are two myths about aging: first, that most of us go through a "midlife crisis"; and, second, that as we grow old, we lose our ambition.

Speculation about the existence of a midlife crisis is a modern phenomenon, a result of the fact that we are now living much longer than our ancestors. Prehistoric humans lived less than three decades. The lifespan of an ancient Greek or Roman was about four decades. In the sixteenth century, one quarter of those born died in the first year, and the second quarter were dead by age sixteen. Most childbearing women died by age thirty. Few people lived to be old, and those who did were studied as curiosities. As recently as 1900, about one half of the men and women who reached the age of twenty did not live on to be sixty-five; now four out of five reach sixty-five.

Midlife is the last uncharted territory in human development; scholars of human development having tended to concentrate on childhood, adolescence, and old age. As a consequence, there still is much ignorance about midlife. Some people view this as a quiet and stable period of life. Professors who teach courses on human development report that it comes as a surprise to many students to recognize that their parents may be having their own growth and adaptation crises. Others believe that midlife is a time of sweeping personality change; that as we move through the adult years, we become transformed in appearance, social life, interests, relationships, ways of experiencing and expressing emotions and desires.

The latter view is most accurate. Many social, biomedical, and psychological events are spread through the midlife period, roughly from age thirty-five to sixty-five. Hormone production levels are dropping, sexual vigor is diminishing, a woman's reproductive life is ending, one is more vulnerable to physical injury and serious illness, facial and body beauty or handsomeness are fading, job opportunities are narrowing, children are not fulfilling parental hopes, there is sudden responsibility for an aging parent, intimate contact with children is lessened, and mortality emerges as a personal issue.

Despite their significance as changes in midlife, these events do not differ in importance from the events taking place in other age periods. Successes and failures can happen at any age. A teenager can be failing in popularity, in trouble with parents, losing a boy or a girl friend, dropped from the team in sports—similarly for childhood and old age. What does seem to happen in midlife specifically, which I think is the basis for speaking about a "crisis," is not the nature of the event but the way in which we manage it.

Two changes get under way in midlife. The first is a change in time perspective—shifting from the indefinite time horizon and long timetables of youth toward the elderly's focus on their finite remaining years. As the sociologist John W. Riley, Jr., reports, contrary to widespread belief, older people do not have a fear of death. We are not afraid of dying or of what will happen to us afterward. What death means is the loss of future achievements and of all the things we wanted to do and felt we could do.

The second change is that during the midlife period the performance/capacity ratio is likely to be at its highest. Where in youth capacity often rises faster than demanded performance, in midlife the performance demands are raised while capacity may remain steady or decline, thus pushing the ratio up toward maximum and inducing stress. In older age, the performance requirements and expectations fall faster than the decline in capacity, and so we return to a lower and less stressful ratio.

The consequence of these changes during midlife is that we begin a major revision in our old, familiar modes of dealing with achievement gaps. Our reserve capacity is shrinking, and we cannot work harder and smarter as we did before. Time is getting scarce, and we can no longer stretch out our timetables. We start to move into new territory, into more changes in aspirations and in goals.

This view of midlife development is supported by research by German and American psychologists. Jochen Brandstädter challenges the idea that middle age is a time of greatest stability and control over one's life. The German people he studies report that they face an increasing number of difficult events that are less under their control. Paul B. Baltes and his research colleagues at the Max Planck Institute for Human Development and Education in Berlin find that when people associate life events with age, the less desirable and less controllable events are ascribed to the older rather than the younger age periods.

Brandstädter has also found that adults are more ready than younger people to say they are willing to change goals and levels of aspiration in situations where they are losing ground. His respondents describe an environment that is becoming more difficult for them and can no longer be managed by creating new methods or by extending timetables. Up to this time, one could make some changes in methods and timetables but has rarely had to give up a major dream in life.

The term *midlife crisis* was used first by the psychoanalyst Elliott Jaques in 1965 when he was writing about "Death and the Mid-Life Crisis." Later in the 1970s, in the work of Daniel J. Levinson and his colleagues (widely popularized in *Passages* by Gail Sheehy), the usage of the term had moved from describing the confrontation with mortality to describing the confrontation with the truth that not all our youthful dreams will be realized— and that the early goals we set aside during our late twenties will re-emerge and will no longer be denied. We ask, "Is this what I meant to be doing at this time in my life? Is this what I really wanted? Was it worth all I had to give up? Do I want to go on doing these things in the years I have left? What are those parts of myself that I had to neglect or suppress?"

By 1990, the term *midlife crisis* was being used to cover many midlife experiences and to justify some strange behavior. It has become a force outside oneself that any middle-aged person can blame, and has taken on a mystical quality. One woman said to me, "My husband says he's going to have it and I'd better get ready for it." Another woman (age forty) told me, "I use it for whatever I feel—mad, depressed, silly, impulsive—'It's mid-life

crisis.' It's way better than calling it 'the menopause' or 'PMS.'"
The psychologist Susan Krauss Whitbourne observes:

> It can be a relief to have a label to give to your unhappiness. . . . If
> you can call it a mid-life crisis, that's much better than having to
> say, 'I'm depressed, I'm neurotic, I'm anxious, I'm miserable with
> my marriage,' or 'I really screwed up.' The label offers a conve-
> nient excuse for irresponsible behavior[,] . . . a quasi-disease to
> blame for infidelity, on-the-job failure, or strained relations with
> one's spouse and children.

The truth is that the "midlife crisis" is more a useful fiction
than a reality. The research thus far reports that few middle-aged
people actually have experiences they would describe with this
term. Fundamental changes in goals and aspirations take place
during these decades naturally, but the desired level of manageable difficulty is restored without a crisis. Changed goals become
familiar over time and gain our commitment, and we enter a new
period of endeavor.

FIRE AT EVENING

A popular view of ambition through life is that there are just so
many jumps in the rabbit, and that these get used up along the
path to old age. But the myth of no ambition in old age will not
hold up. A truer picture is that the rabbit keeps jumping right
through life, but the jumps are not as high and not as far as in the
early years. The drive for growth and mastery is still there, but
not as obviously as before.

I believe we make two basic errors when we consider ambition
in older people. One is that we mistake their greater calmness
about winning and losing—which comes from long experience
with these events through their lives—with a lack of interest in
what happens.

Consider a first loss in childhood. The game of marbles is
ancient and, in one form or another, almost universal to human
cultures. Afghan boys today roll small stones into a ring to knock
out and win the stones of other boys. American children shoot

polished balls of glass or agate. Losing your marbles is a life event shared by tens of millions in early childhood. For most of them, it is the first time they have irrevocably lost something that is theirs. Before this, the game is played at home with a brother or a sister, where the parents say it is just for fun, "not for keeps," and the marbles are returned after the game. The first game of playing for keeps outside the home, where the child is not protected by the special family rules, will bring the pain of real loss and of having to deal with it. The song, "Little Man, You've Had a Busy Day" has this verse: "Johnny won your marbles, Tell you what we'll do; Daddy will buy you new ones right away." This might happen once, in the transition to the real world, but then the child coming home with an empty marble bag learns that this time he or she does not get the marbles back. We say, "Winners keepers, losers weepers." The child is told to toughen up and try again, and sent out to play another day.

Winning or losing events has less impact if one has a base of prior experience. It takes a large win or loss to affect older people as strongly as a small win or loss does a child. We can contrast youth and age in this way. Biomedical scientists studying differences between young and old people use a "tilt bed" to put people in unusual positions, such as feet up and head down, and see what happens to their blood pressure. When brought back to normal position, the younger subjects recover their normal blood pressure much more quickly—almost instantly—than the older adults do. But, in dealing with success and failure in life, the reverse may be true. The youth may be more puzzled, less able to recognize and analyze, and have less of a mental map in which to place an event, and thus a harder time managing the wins or losses than may the older, more experienced adult—who seems, in comparison, calm, cool, and wise.

It is also a mistake, in respect to ambition in older people, to assume that the diminished endeavors of one's later years are not as meaningful as the grand plans of one's youth. The level of performance may decline on an absolute scale, but it remains pegged at the level of just manageable difficulty. There is a contrast here with some of the biomedical processes in our bodies. For instance, the ratio of hormone production to metabolism remains steady, although both may drop by 20 percent as we get older. Other ratios like this hold steady, even though declining in an absolute sense. But here is the great difference: as our biomedical processes decline, we may feel less healthy and become ill; while in the psychological realm, living at the level of just manageable difficulty provides happiness just as great as it was in youth and midlife.

The fire may burn lower, but it burns on, as in Paul Klee's painting *Fire at Evening*, where the hot red-orange center—the life force—still suffuses fifty or more small spaces of striving, struggle, and resolution. The image of "old people" as aimless, vegetating humans misses what is really going on. All are working on something; you just have to ask them. And when you ask, "What are you working on?" they have a list almost as long as any thirty-year-old's. And even the very old people, beyond the wheelchair races and the shuffleboard contests, have a growing edge: to look good, to care for oneself, to walk to the kitchen, visit with friends, sit outdoors, be close to their family, hold someone's hand.

When we search into what older people want and what they are doing, we make a discovery. The familiar channels for growth and mastery in their earlier years now are closed to them, and they must find new challenges. At the same time, at this point in life they are more free of social controls. They can go after what interests them instead of what society says they must do. Individual differences increase. They tend to take up eccentric, even bizarre, pursuits—the fireworks display of ambition in an aging population.

From the baby boy in the crib, looking up at the mobile dangling above, smiling while he makes it move by shifting his head on the sensitized pillow; to the two-year-old girl shouting, "Me do it myself"; to youths filled with dreams of grand accomplishments; to a one-hundred-year-old man feeling with his hands the texture of the earth in his window boxes, caring for his flowers— we look for the challenges that are right for us, for what we can just manage, and in this way form and shape our lives and conduct our many missions.

Notes

For the discussion in the prologue and elsewhere in the book, I have drawn freely from my article, "Losing and Winning," *Psychology Today*, September 1988, pp. 48–52.

Chapter 1: Our Drive for Growth and Mastery

Page
9   D. A. Hamburg, G.V. Coelho, and J. E. Adams, "Steps Toward a Synthesis of Biological and Social Perspectives," *Coping and Adaptation* (New York: Basic Books, 1974), pp. 13, 403-40.

10   James A. Michener, quoted in Gilbert Brim, "Losing and Winning," *Psychology Today*, September 1988, pp. 48–52.

11   Ellen Langer and Judith Rodin, "The Effects of Choice and Enhanced Personal Responsibility for the Aged: A Field Experiment in an Institutional Setting," *Journal of Personality and Social Psychology* 34 (1976): 191–98.

11   On studies of job satisfaction, see Robert L. Kahn, *Work and Health* (New York: John Wiley, 1991).

11   Mihaly Csikszentmihaly told me about the assembly-line worker, personal communication.

12   John Skow, "Risking It All," *Time* 122 (29 August 1983): 52–56.

13   Rosdail's story reported by S. Carr, "Jesse Hart Rosdail Has Visited 143 of the World's 147 Countries," *New York Times,* 11 November 1973.

13   Adachi's creations described by S. Rimer, "Perfection of 1,000 Chrysanthemums Reveals Japanese Spirit in the Bronx," *New York Times,* 31 October 1983.

13   The "ultimate marathon" described by J. R. Moskin, "The Ultimate Marathon," in Health/Spectator/London, June 1985, quoted from *The Press* (Christchurch, 16 June 1985).

14   Alexander's achievements reported by Jon Nordheimar, "Top-of-the-Line Chicken Soup," *New York Times,* 20 April 1987, C12.

14   Plato, *The Republic* 1 (trans. Benjamin Jowett [Chicago: Henry Regnery, 1948]).

14   The billionaires described by Marshall Loeb, "The Editor's Desk"—"The Billionaires," *Fortune,* 12 October 1987, p. 4.

15   Games discussed by Terry Orlick, *The Second Cooperative Sports and Games Book* (New York: Pantheon, 1982).

16   W. H. Davies, "Ambition," *The Poems of W. H. Davies* (New York: Oxford University Press, 1935), p. 408, originally published 1929.

16   Joseph Conrad, *Under Western Eyes,* Boris Ford, ed. (New York: Penguin Books, 1986), part 3, p. 3.

16   William Shakespeare, *King Henry VI,* part I, 2.5. 123.

17   Janet T. Spence, "Achievement American Style: The Rewards and Costs of Individualism," *American Psychologist* 40 (1986): 1285–95.

18   Ayn Rand, *Atlas Shrugged* (New York: Random House, 1957).

18   The Confucian saying from "Chinese Proverbs Under Party Fire," *New York Times,* 1 September 1974, p. 8.

19   Epicurus, "Vatican Sayings" 35, *Letters, Principal Doctrines, and Vatican Sayings* (trans. Russell M. Geer [New York: Macmillan, 1964]).

20   David A. Hamburg, *Coping and Adaptation* (New York: Basic Books, 1974), p. 407.

21   The goals of American college freshmen from John J. Conger, "Hostages to Fortune: Youth, Values, and the Public Interest," *American Psychologist,* April 1988, pp. 291–300.

22   Women's aspirations from Kenneth Spenner and David L. Featherman, "Achievement Ambitions," *Annual Review of Sociology,* vol. 4 (Palo Alto, Calif. Annual Reviews, 1978).

23   On the lack of difference in achievement striving, see Henry N. Riccuti, *A Review of Procedural Variations in Level of Aspiration Studies,* Research Bulletin 51–24 (San Antonio:

Human Resources Research Center, 1951); and Douglas G. Schultz, *The Relationship Between Group Experimental Level of Aspiration Measures and Self-Estimates of Personality,* Project Designation NR 151–113 (Princeton: Educational Testing Service, May 1954).

23   On gender differences, see Aletha C. Huston, "Sex-Typing," in P. H. Mussen, ed., *Handbook of Child Psychology,* IV: *Socialization, Personality, and Social Development* (New York: John Wiley, 1983), pp. 404–05.

23   "On wheeled vehicles . . ." from Eleanor E. Maccoby, "Gender Differentiation: Explanatory Viewpoints," address delivered to the American Psychological Society (June 1990).

23   The Center for Creative Leadership quote from A. M. Morrison, R. P. White, and El Van Velsor, "The Narrow Band," *Issues and Observations* 7 (2 [Spring 1987], Center for Creative Leadership, Greensboro, N.C.).

24   Research on men and women from Alice S. Rossi, "Life Span Theories and Women's Lives," *Signs: Journal of Women in Culture and Society* 6(1) [Autumn 1980]: 4–32.

25   Information on the Swedish Twin Registry reported by Gerald McClearn, personal communication, May 1987.

25   For individual differences in human genes, see Richard Lewontin, *Human Diversity* (New York: W. H. Freeman, 1984), p. 179.

27   Charlie Smith, *The Lives of the Dead* (New York: Linden Press/Simon & Schuster, 1990).

Chapter 2: Looking for Just Manageable Difficulties

Page
29   Nicholas Hobbs, "A Natural History of an Idea: Project Re-Ed," in J. M. Kaufmann and C. D. Lewis, eds., *Teaching Children with Behavior Disorders* (Columbus, Ohio.: Charles E. Merrill, 1974), pp. 164–65. See also Nicholas Hobbs, "The Art of Getting Students into Trouble," in Lawrence E. Dennis, Joseph F. Kaufmann, eds., *The College and the Student* (Washington, D.C.: American Council on Education, 1966), pp. 202–5; and Nicholas Hobbs, "The Psychologist as Administrator," *Journal of Clinical Psychology* 25 (July 1959):237–40.

30   The experiment on memory reported by H. Meltzer, "Individual Differences in Forgetting Pleasant and Un-

pleasant Experiences, *Journal of Educational Psychology* 21 (1930):399–409.

31   Alexis de Tocqueville, *Democracy in America*, vol I (Chicago: Henry Regnery, 1951).

32   Studies of AT&T executives in D. W. Bray, R. J. Campbell, and D. L. Grant, *Formative Years in Business* (New York: John Wiley & Sons, 1974).

32   Laurence J. Peter, *The Peter Principle: Why Things Always Go Wrong* (New York: William Morrow, 1971).

33   Harold F. Clark, *Economic Theory and Correct Occupational Distribution*, Léon Stein, ed. (Salem, N.H.: Ayer, 1977, reprint of 1931 ed.).

35   The Roper Poll in "Fast Times," *Harper's*, February 1985, p. 18.

36   Arthur Mizener, "Scott Fitzgerald and the Top Girl," *Atlantic Monthly* 207 (March 1961): 55–60.

37   John Barth, *Giles Goat Boy* (New York: Fawcett, 1978).

38   The survey of high school students in O. G. Brim, Jr., et al., *American Beliefs and Attitudes about Intelligence* (New York: Russell Sage Foundation, 1969).

38   Deborah Phillips, "The Illusion of Incompetence Among Academically Competent Children," *Child Development* 55 (1984): 2000–2016.

44   Classical theories of happiness are discussed in R. B. Brandt, "Happiness," *Encyclopaedia of Philosophy* (New York: Macmillan and Free Press, 1967), vol. III, pp. 413–14; and in A. Edel, "Happiness and Pleasure," in P. P. Wiener, ed., *Dictionary of the History of Ideas, Studies of Selected Pivotal Ideas* (New York: Charles Scribner, 1982), vol. II, pp. 374–87.

44   James Boswell, *Life of Samuel Johnson* (February 1766) (New York: McGraw-Hill, 1964).

45   Sarah Orne Jewett, "A White Heron," in C. Fadiman, ed., *Reading I've Liked* (New York: Simon & Schuster, 1943), pp. 406–7.

45   The Ethiopian desert described in "The Forbidden Desert of the Danakil," episode 702, first aired 6 March 1988, Public Broadcasting System, WNET, New York, NY.

45   R. B. Brandt, "Happiness," in Paul Edwards, ed., *Encyclopaedia of Philosophy* (New York: Macmillan and Free Press, 1967), vol. 3, pp. 413–14.

46   Rona Jaffe, *The Fame Game* (Cutchogue, N.Y.: Buccaneer Books, 1976, reprint of 1969 ed).

46   On happiness and socio-economic background, see Norman M.

Bradburn, *The Structure of Psychological Well-Being* (Chicago: Aldine, 1969).

47   Studies on education and subjective well-being reviewed by R. A. Witter, et al., "Education and Subjective Well-Being: A Meta-Analysis," *Educational Evaluation and Policy Analysis* 6 (2 [Summer 1984]): 165–73.

47   The Canadian Survey in I. McDowell and E. Praught, "On the Measurement of Happiness," *American Journal of Epidemiology* 116 (6 [December 1982]):949–58.

47   The effects of race reported by Philip E. Converse, A. Campbell, and W. Rodgers, *The Quality of American Life* (New York: Russell Sage Foundation, 1976).

48   The seven national surveys from E. F. Borgatta and R. G. Foss, "Correlates of Age," The NORC General Social Survey, *Research on Aging* 1 (2 [June 1979]):253–72. See also A. R. Herzog, W. L. Rodgers, and J. Woodworth, "Subjective Well-Being among Different Age Groups," Research Report Series, Survey Research Center, Institute for Social Research, University of Michigan (1982).

48   On the problems of the old, see Felicia Lee, "Getting Old Not As Bad As We Think," *USA Today,* 19 November 1984, p. A-1.

48   For correlation of income and happiness, see Campbell, Converse, and Rodgers, *Quality.* See also Diane Swandrow, "Who Is Happiest?" *Psychology Today,* July/August 1989, p. 39.

48   Aristotle, "Nicomachean Ethics," 1.8 tr. J. A. K. Thomson (Chicago, IL: Henry Regnery Co. [Regnery/Gateway, Inc.], 1948).

48   "Money Isn't Everything," by Richard Rodgers and Oscar Hammerstein, Jr. (Williamson Music Co., 1947).

48   The national surveys of young American children reported by N. Zill, *America's Children: Happy, Healthy, and Insecure,* unpublished manuscript, Foundation for Child Development, New York City, 1984.

Chapter 3: Did We Win or Lose?

Page
53   David Mamet, *Glengarry Glen Ross* (New York: Ever, 1988 [imprint of Grove]).

54   The Olympic boxer quoted by Frederick C. Klein, "No Medal

for Andrew: The Nine-Minute Olympics," *Wall Street Journal*, 2 August 1984.

55   Sara Teasdale, "The Long Hill," in Louis Untermeyer, ed., *Modern American Poetry and Modern British Poetry* (New York: Harcourt Brace, 1950), p. 286. (From: "Frame and Shadow," 1920; England Revised Edition, 1922).

57   Konishiki reported on by David E. Sanger, "American Is Crowned Japan's Sumo Champ," *New York Times*, 24 November 1989, A-241.

57   Pete Dawkins reported on by G. Vecsey, "Pete Dawkins Remembers," *New York Times*, 30 November 1984.

58   This discussion on foundations draws freely from O. G. Brim, Jr., "Do We Know What We Are Doing?" in F. Heimann, ed., *The Future of Foundations* (Englewood Cliffs, N.J.: Prentice-Hall, 1972).

61   Sisela Bok, *Lying: Moral Choice in Public and Private Life* (New York: Random House, 1979, 1989). See also Sisela Bok, *Secrets: On the Ethics of Concealment and Revelation* (New York: Pantheon, 1983, 1989).

61   Edith Wharton, *Four Novelettes by Edith Wharton* (New York: Charles Scribner, 1970), p. 38.

61   Paul Juhl, "Japanese Rejection Slip," *Survival* (a Civil Defense publication in Alberta, Canada, 1963). Reprinted in *Authors Guild Bulletin*.

62   On organizational management, see R. E. Kaplan, W. H. Drath, and J. R. Kofodimos, "Power and Getting Criticism," *Issues and Observations* Greensboro, N.C.: Center for Creative Leadership 4 (3 [August 1984]). See also R. E. Kaplan, W. H. Drath, and J. R. Kofodimos, *Beyond Ambition: How Driven Managers Can Lead Better and Live Better* (San Francisco: Jossey-Bass, in press).

64   Heywood Broun, "Sports for Art's Sake," *Pieces of Hate, and Other Enthusiasms* (New York: New Playwrights Network, 1922).

64   John Greenleaf Whittier, "Maud Muller" (stanza 53), in William Cullen Bryant, ed., *Library of Poetry and Song* (New York: Doubleday, Page, 1925), vol. I, p. 158.

Chapter 4: Planning the Next Actions

Page
66   Surveys of beliefs about the future reported by M. Konner, "Why the Reckless Survive," *Sciences*, May/June 1987.

67 Lionel Tiger, *Optimism: The Biology of Hope* (New York: Simon & Schuster, 1979).

67 Research on children from Susan Harter, "Processes Underlying the Construction, Maintenance and Enhancement of the Self-Concept in Children," in J. Suls and A. Greenwald, *Psychological Perspectives on the Self,* vol. 3 (Hillsdale, N.J.: Lawrence Erlbaum, 1985).

67 Studies of depression and positive and optimistic thinking from Shelley E. Taylor, *Positive Illusions: Creative Self-Deception and the Healthy Mind* (New York: Basic Books, 1989).

68 "Self-handicapping" from E. E. Jones and S. Berglas, "Control of Attributions About the Self Through Self-handicapping Strategies: The Appeal of Alcohol and the Role of Underachievement," *Personality and Social Psychology Bulletin* 4 (2 [1978]): 200–206.

70 Research on lottery behavior in Ellen J. Langer, "The Illusion of Control," *Journal of Personality and Social Psychology* 32 (1975): 311–28.

72 Cartoon: by Al Ross, "It is *not* in the lap of the gods . . . ," *New Yorker,* 3 June 1985, p. 106.

72 Phyllis Rose, "Hers" column, *New York Times,* 1 March 1984, C-2.

73 On "risk preference," see Ward Edwards, and Amos Tversky, eds., *Decision Making: Selected Readings* (Harmondsworth, England: Penguin Books, 1967). See also Detlov von Winterfeldt and Ward Edwards, *Decision Analysis and Behavioral Research* (New York: Cambridge University Press, 1986).

74 Kenneth Prewitt, personal communication, October 1983.

76 Nick Wayte, *Seconds* (Berkeley, Calif.: Small Press Distribution, 1969).

76 Ken Grimwood, *Replay,* Damaris Rowland, ed. (New York: Berkley, 1988).

76 "Peggy Sue Got Married," movie, Tri-Star, 1988.

76 Rules on second chances from David A. Goslin and Nancy Bordier, "Recordkeeping in Elementary and Secondary Schools," in Wheeler, Stanton, *Files & Dossiers in American Life* (New York: Russell Sage Foundation, 1969). See also Russell Sage Foundation, *Guidelines for the Collection, Maintenance and Dissemination of Pupil Records,* report of a conference on the ethical and legal aspects of school record-keeping (New York: Russell Sage Foundation, 1970).

77 The five best sellers from "5 Books That Made Fools & Millionaires," *New York Post,* 6 March 1990.

Chapter 5: Can We Make the Change?

Page

79   Jeremiah 13:23.

79   The discussion in this chapter draws freely from O. G. Brim, Jr., and J. Kagan, eds., "Constancy and Change: A View of the Issues," *Constancy and Change in Human Development* (Cambridge, Mass.: Harvard University Press, 1980), pp. 1–25.

80   On the molecules in our body, see Caleb E. Finch, *Longevity, Senescence, and the Genome* (Chicago: University of Chicago Press, 1990).

82   Jan Morris, *Conundrum* (New York: Harcourt Brace, 1974).

84   For images of ourselves, see H. Markus and E. Wurf, "The Dynamic of Self Concept: A Social Psychological Perspective," *Annual Review of Psychology* 38 (1987): 299–337.

84   The survey of midlife executives in T. D. Kemper, L. S. Cottrell, Jr., and N. Goodman, "Self, Roles, and Others, A Study in Social Psychology," unpublished manuscript, Russell Sage Foundation, New York, 1970.

84   *On the Waterfront,* Columbia Pictures, 1954.

84   Aldous Huxley, *Brave New World* (New York: Harper & Row, 1960), pp. vii–viii.

84   Brendan Gill, *Here at the New Yorker* (New York: Carroll & Graf, Inc., 1987), p. 77.

85   For images of ourselves today and in the future, see R. W. Bortner and D. F. Hultsch, "Patterns of Subjective Deprivation in Adulthood," *Developmental Psychology* 10 (4 [1974]): 534–45.

87   *Shoeless Joe* quote in Daniel Okrent review, *New York Times,* 25 July 1982, G-10. See also *Field of Dreams,* movie, Universal Studios, 1990.

91   Bernice L. Neugarten, "The Study of Aging and Human Development," paper presented at Symposium "Race, Class, Socialization and the Life Cycle," University of Chicago, 10 October 1983.

Chapter 6: How Free Are We to Act?

Page

93   On socialization, see O. G. Brim, Jr., "Personality Development as Role-Learning," in I. Iscoe and H. Stevenson, eds.,

Personality Development in Children (Austin: University of Texas Press, 1960), pp. 127–59.

95 Roger Simon, "Winners, Losers—Each a Miss America," *Extra*, June 1980, pp. 11–12.

95 Michael Jackson, interview on CBS Evening News, 8 February 1984.

95 "The Monastery," ABC-TV "News Close-up," 20 August 1981.

95 The cartoon by Dean Vietor, "Good evening . . . ," *New Yorker*, 21 April 1986, p. 54.

96 Robert L. Kahn, "Aging and Social Support," in Matilda White Riley, ed., *Aging from Birth to Death: Interdisciplinary Perspectives* (Boulder, Col.: Westview Press, 1979), pp. 77–92.

96 *New Yorker* cartoons: Saul Steinberg, "Dog," 25 April 1970, p. 43; Mick Stevens, "Roget's Bronto," 4 March 1985, p. 52; Charles Barsotti, "Lone Wolf," 27 January 1986, p. 31.

97 Phil Meihre, ABC-TV broadcast of the XIV Winter Olympics, 19 February 1984.

98 Alfred C. Kinsey, Wardell B. Pomeroy, and Clyde E. Martin, *Sexual Behavior in the Human Male* (Philadelphia: W. B. Saunders, 1948).

100 Chinese scholars described in catalogue for Asia Society show, "The Chinese Scholars Studio: Artistic Life in the Late Ming Era" (15 October 1987–3 January 1988).

100 Ronald Sukenick, "Up From the Garret: Success Then and Now," *New York Times Book Review*, 27 January 1985.

100 Franklin Baumer, personal communication, 1942. Robert Crane, personal communication, 1962.

101 Robert Wilson, *The American Poet: A Role Investigation* (New York: Garland, 1990).

101 Figures on social groups from A. Gartner and F. Riessman, "Lots of Helping Hands," *New York Times*, 19 February 1980.

101 Helen R. F. Ebaugh, *Becoming an Ex: The Process of Role Exit* (Chicago: University of Chicago Press, 1988).

102 Hendrik Hertzberg, "The Education of Mr. Smith," *Esquire*, February 1986, pp. 37–38.

102 Studies of business managers in D. A. Saunders, "Executive Discontent," in S. Nosow and W. H. Form, eds., *Man, Work and Society* (New York: Basic Books, 1962).

102 On aging of managers, see Curt Tausky, and Robert Dubin, "Career Anchorage: Managerial Mobility Motivations," *American Sociological Review* 30 (1965): 725–35.

102   Robert R. Faulkner, "Coming of Age in Organizations—A Comparative Study of Career Contingencies and Adult Socialization," *Sociology of Work and Occupations* 1 (2 [1974]): 131–73.

103   W. J. Tilley, *Masters of the Situation* (New York: N. D. Thompson, 1889), p. 765.

104   Harry Helsen, *Adaptation-Level Theory* (New York: Harper & Row, 1964).

105   National surveys from Jim Henderson, "How Rich Is Rich?" *U.S.A. Today,* 12 October 1984, p. A-1.

106   Wilson quoted in "Actress at Large Seeks Inner Resources," *New York Times,* 29 July 1984.

106   *Boston Globe,* 4 November 1986.

106   Hemingway's son quoted in Gerald Clarke, "The Sons Almost Rise," *Fame,* September 1989, pp. 100–111.

107   Robert K. Merton, and Alice S. Kitt (Rossi), "Contributions to the Theory of Reference Group Behavior," in R. K. Merton and P. F. Lazarsfeld, eds. *Contributions in Social Research: Studies in the Scope and Method of "The American Soldier"* (Glencoe, Il.: Free Press, 1950), pp. 40–105.

107   Samuel A. Stouffer, et al., *The American Soldier: Adjustment during Army Life,* vol. I (Manhattan, Kan.: MA/AH Publishing, division of Sunflower University Press, Kansas State University, 1949).

107   Ambrose G. Bierce, *The Devil's Dictionary* (Mattituck, N.Y.: Amereon, reprint of 1911 ed.).

107   Russell Baker, "On Top in Wampum," *New York Times,* 23 August 1977, p. A-35.

Chapter 7: The Sequence of Transformation

Page
111   On "human learning," see T. H. Leahey and R. J. Harris, *Human Learning,* 2nd ed. (Englewood Cliffs, N.J.: Prentice Hall, 1989); and H. C. Ellis and R. R. Hung, *Fundamentals of Human Memory and Cognition,* 4th ed. (Dubuque, Iowa: William C. Brown, 1989).

113   The study of fired workers in Ronald C. Kessler, J. B. Turner, and J. S. House, "Factors Facilitating Adjustment to Unemployment: Implications for Intervention," *American Journal of Community Psychology,* in press.

114   Gary T. Marx, "Reflections on Academic Success and Failure: Making It, Forsaking It, Reshaping It," in B. M. Berger, ed., *Authors of Their Own Lives: Intellectual Autobiographies of Twenty American Sociologists* (Berkeley: University of California Press, 1990), pp. 260–84, quote on p. 264.

115   The social psychologists are R. Janoff-Bulman and P. Brickman, "Expectations and What People Learn From Failure," in N. T. Feather, ed., *Expectations and Actions* (Hillsdale, N.J.: Lawrence Erlbaum, 1982), pp. 207–37.

Chapter 8: Changing Timetables

Page
119   On time, see E. R. Leach, *Rethinking Anthropology* (London: Athalone, 1961).

119   T. J. Cottle and S. L. Klineberg, *The Present of Things Future* (New York: Free Press, 1974), p. 71.

120   For the "flow experience," see Mihaly Csikszentmihalyi, *Flow: The Psychology of Optimal Experience* (New York: Harper & Row, 1990).

121   Robert K. Merton, "Socially Expected Durations: A Case Study of Concept Formation in Sociology," in W. W. Powell and R. Robbins, eds., *Conflict and Consensus: A Festschrift for Lewis A. Coser* (New York: Free Press, 1984), pp. 262–83.

124   On Wall Street, see R. G. Eccles, "Doing Deals: Investment Banks at Work," *Harvard Business School Bulletin,* October 1988.

125   D. K. Simonton, "Age and Outstanding Achievement: What Do We Know After a Century of Research?" *Psychological Bulletin* 104 (2 [1988]):251–67.

125   Criticism of research studies in Harriet Zuckerman and Robert K. Merton, "Age, Aging, and Age Structure in Science," in Matilda White Riley, Marilyn Johnson, and Anne Foner, eds., *Aging and Society,* vol. 3 (New York: Russell Sage Foundation, 1972), pp. 292–56.

126   Description of policeman's role in advertisement for Patrolmen's Benevolent Association, New York City.

126   Robert R. Faulkner, "Coming of Age in Organizations—A Comparative Study of Career Contingencies and Adult Socialization," *Sociology of Work and Occupations* 1 (2 [1974]):131–73.

127   Moravia interview from A. M. de Dominicus and B. Johnson,

"Alberto Moravia," in M. Cowley, ed., *Writers at Work: The Paris Review Interviews,* First Series (New York: Viking Press, 1967), pp. 211–29.

128   Irwin Shaw, "The Eighty-Yard Run," in *Welcome to the City, and Other Stories* (New York: Random House, 1942).

128   Robert Lipsyte, "The Athlete's Losing Game," *New York Times Magazine,* 30 November 1986.

128   M. Gross, "Carrie Fisher, Novelist, Looks Back at the Edge," *New York Times,* 14 August 1987.

129   Robert Browning, "The Last Duchess," *Poems by Robert Browning* (New York: Thomas Y. Crowell, 1896), p. 2.

129   Berlin quoted by William Morehouse, "Berlin Baedeker," *Theatre Arts* 42 (February 1958):27–29.

129   Garbo quoted by John Lahr, "The World's Most Sensational Absence," *New York Times Book Review,* 24 June 1990.

129   Alfred Tennyson, "In Memoriam," part XXVII, stanza 4, originally published 1850.

129   Ken Grimwood, *Replay,* Damaris Rowland, ed. (New York: Berkley, 1988), pp. 107–8.

130   Duke Ellington quoted in his obituary by John S. Wilson, *New York Times,* 25 May 1974, p. A-1.

130   Santmyer's success described by E. McDowell, "Happy End for a Novelist's 50-Year Effort," *New York Times,* 12 January 1984.

130   Churchill described by Frank Harris, *Contemporary Portraits* (third series) (Mellwood, N.Y.: Reprints & Periodicals, Division of Kraus Organization, 1920).

132   On Gauguin, see H. Gold, "Paul Gauguin," *Islands,* June 1984, pp. 59–60.

132   Results of 1987 stock market crash in Meg Cox, "Wall Street Yuppies Thrive But Show 'New Humility,'" *Wall Street Journal,* 24 October 1988, p. C-1, quotes on p. C-16.

133   Frank R. Westie, "Academic Expectations for Professional Immortality: A Study of Legitimation," *Sociological Forum,* Summer 1972, pp. 1–25.

133   Belief in Heaven reported by A. L. Goldman, "Religion Notes," *New York Times,* 23 March 1991.

134   Cartoon by Donald Reilly, "Not now, I've got too many things . . . ," *New Yorker,* 19 May 1975, p. 46.

135   This first textbook from M. I. Finley and H. W. Pleket, *The Olympic Games; The First Thousand Years* (London: Chatto & Windus, 1976).

136   *Chariots of Fire,* TCF/Allied Stars/Enigma, 1981.

139   Arthur Miller, *Death of a Salesman* (Penguin, 1976).

139   Holloway's story reported in R. Suro, "Love, Ambition and the
       Price for a Child's Success," *New York Times,* 17 March
       1991.

140   Japanese executives final thoughts in Jack Burton, "Jet Diary—
       'I'm Sure I Won't Make It,'" *U.S.A. Today,* 19 August
       1985, sec. A, p. 1.

Chapter 9: Changing Levels of Aspiration

Page

143   John Galsworthy, "The Wine Horn Mountain."

144   For studies on risk-taking behavior, see Henry N. Riccuti, *A
       Review of Procedural Variations in Level of Aspiration Studies,*
       research bulletin 51-24 (San Antonio: Human Resources
       Research Center, 1951); and Henry N. Riccuti and Douglas
       G. Schultz, *The Relationship Between Group Experimental Level
       of Aspiration Measures and Self-Estimates of Personality,* project
       designation NR 151-113 (Princeton, N.J.: Educational
       Testing Service, May 1954).

145   On parental aspirations, see L. I. Pearlin, M. R. Yarrow, and H.
       A. Scarr, "Unintended Effects of Parental Aspirations: The
       Case of Children's Cheating," *American Journal of Sociology*
       73 (July 1967): 73–83.

145   Daniel Defoe, *The Life and Strange Surprising Adventures of
       Robinson Crusoe, of York, Mariner* (New York: Grosset &
       Dunlap, 1946).

146   Robert Browning, "Andrea Del Sarto," *Men and Women 1855,*
       Paul Turner, ed. (New York: Oxford University Press,
       1972).

146   *Yiddish Proverbs,* Hanan J. Ayalti, ed. (New York: Schocken [a
       division of Random House], 1987).

146   Carey reported on in "Unsmiling Carey Offers Apology," *New
       York Times,* 3 August 1984, pp. B–14.

146   Harriet Zuckerman, *Scientific Elite: Nobel Laureates in the United
       States* (New York: Free Press, 1977).

147   *Rocky,* United Artists, 1976.

147   Michel de Montaigne, "Of Cannibals," in *The Complete Essays,*
       trans. Donald Frame (Stanford, Calif.: University of Stanford
       Press, 1958).

147   M. I. Finley and H. W. Pleket, *The Olympic Games; The First*

Thousand Years (London: Chatto & Windus, 1976), pp. 20–22; quotes on pp. 22, 20, and 21, respectively.

148   Game theory discussed by Martin Shubik, *Game Theory in the Social Sciences: Concepts and Solutions* (Cambridge, Mass. MIT Press, 1984).

149   Cartoon by Gahan Wilson, "More," *New Yorker,* 11 February 1985, p. 53.

150   Perry reported on by M. Janofsky, "Refrigerator Turns on a Hungry Public," *New York Times,* 10 November, 1985.

150   Quotes by and about Perry in D. Anderson, "Oysters in Season," *New York Times,* 23 January 1986.

150   Quote on the pathological gambler from C. P. Peck, "Risk-Taking Behavior and Compulsive Gambling," *American Psychologist,* April 1986, pp. 461–65.

150   Sanders quoted by M. Kernan, "Lawrence Sanders Stays Unprejudiced by Reality," *International Herald Tribune,* 9 September 1985, p. 20.

151   Burton quoted by Bob Greene, "When Fame Is Overnight," *Chicago Tribune,* 16 May 1978, sec. 2, p. 1.

151   The study of lottery winners in P. Brickman, D. Coates, and R. Janoff-Bulman, "Lottery Winners and Accident Victims: Is Happiness Relative?" *Journal of Personality and Social Psychology* 36 (8 [1978]: 917–27. The best general reference to lottery-winning effects is H. R. Kaplan, *Lottery Winners* (Harper & Row, 1978), p. 67.

151   On activities of most lottery winners, see Kaplan, *Lottery Winners.*

152   Lottery winners quoted by Jerry D. LeBlanc, and Rena Dictor LeBlanc, *Suddenly Rich* (New York: Prentice-Hall, 1978).

152   The Canadian woman winner reported in "Lotto Winner Accused of Plotting Murder of Son's Wife," *New York Times* (from Associated Press), 1 August, 1988, p. A-12.

153   The scholar is Kaplan, *Lottery Winners.*

154   The California study in John A. Clausen, "The Life Course of Individuals," in M. W. Riley, M. Johnson, and A. Foner, eds., *Aging and Society, III: A Sociology of Age Stratification* (New York: Russell Sage Foundation, 1972).

154   Robert R. Faulkner, "Coming of Age in Organizations—A Comparative Study of Career Contingencies and Adult Socialization," *Sociology of Work and Occupations* 1 (2 [1974]): 131–73.

154   D. W. Bray, R. J. Campbell, and D. L. Grant, *Formative Years in Business* (New York: John Wiley, 1974), pp. 177–78.

Chapter 10: Changing Goals

Page
158   K. A. Ericsson, C. Tesch-Römer, and R. Th. Krampe, "The Role of Practice and Motivation in the Acquisition of Expert-Level Performance in Real Life: An Empirical Evaluation of a Theoretical Framework," in M. J. A. Howe, ed., *Encouraging the Development of Exceptional Abilities and Talents* (Leicester, England: British Psychological Society, 1990).

158   Ramanujan described by Gina Kolata, "Remembering a 'Magical Genius,'" *Science* 236 (19 June 1987):1519–21.

158   "Madman Honored for Tree Planting," *South China Morning Post*, 18 March 1984.

159   The poet is Nina Cassian, "Greed," in "Four Poems," *New Yorker*, 8 January 1990, p. 30.

159   The personality test in J. C. Hansen and D. P. Campbell, "Strong Interest Inventory of the Strong Vocational Interest Blanks" (Palo Alto, Calif.: Consulting Psychologists Press, 1933, 1985).

159   For studies on prestige ranking, see Alex Inkeles and Peter H. Rossi, "National Comparisons of Occupational Prestige," *American Journal of Sociology* 61 (January 1956):329–39; and Donald Treiman, Robert W. Hodge, and Peter H. Rossi, "A Comparative Study of Occupational Prestige," in R. Bendix and S. M. Lipset, eds., *Class, Status and Power*, 2nd ed. (Glencoe, Ill.: Free Press, 1960), pp. 309–21.

159   E. J. Walsh, *Dirty Work, Race and Self-Esteem,* University of Michigan, Institute of Labor and Industrial Relations, Ann Arbor, 1975.

160   W. H. Auden, *The Collected Poetry of W. H. Auden* (New York: Random House, 1945), p. 198.

164   Steven Berglas, "The Success Syndrome," *American Health: Fitness of Mind and Body* 8 (April 1989): 56.

165   Chris Chase, "First Lady of Talk," *Life,* 14 July 1972.

165   Murphy's Sixth Corollary on a calendar produced by A. Bloch, Price/Stern/Sloan, Inc., Los Angeles, Calif. (1985).

166   The young man reported by Connie Bruck, "Billion-Dollar Mind," *New Yorker,* 7 August 1989, pp. 76–77.

166   "Another woman" in M. G. Warner, "Rise of Consumer Agency's Chief: A Tale of Ambition in Washington," *Wall Street Journal,* 1 July 1982.

166   Faulkner quoted by J. S. vanden Heuvel, "William Faulkner," in M. Cowley, ed., *Writers at Work: The Paris Review*

Interviews, first series (New York: Viking, 1967), p. 123.

167 On Spock and Fonda, see J. Martin, "Nice Work," *Vanity Fair,* February 1984, pp. 24–27.

168 Helen Vendler, review of Allen Ginsburg, *The Fall of America, New York Times,* 15 April 1973, p. G-1.

168 Pollock in Jeffrey Potter, *To a Violent Grave: An Oral Biography of Jackson Pollock* (New York: G. P. Putnam, 1987).

168 Robert Frost, "The Armful," *Collected Poems of Robert Frost* (Garden City, N.Y.: Garden City Publishing, 1936), p. 343.

169 Bourgin reported on by L. Greenhouse, "After 45 Years, Vindication for Scholar," *New York Times,* 22 April 1988.

171 The discussion in this section draws freely from O. G. Brim, Jr., "Theories of the Male Mid-Life Crisis," *Counseling Psychologist* 6 (1 American Psychological Association, 1976): 2–9.

172 In respect to men in midlife, see M. W. Lear, "Is There a Male Menopause?" *New York Times Magazine,* 28 January 1973.

172 John W. Riley, Jr., "Dying and the Meanings of Death: Sociological Inquiries," *Annual Review of Sociology,* 1983.

173 Jochen Brandstädter, "Personal Self-Regulation of Development: Cross-Sequential Analyses of Development-Related Control Beliefs and Emotions," *Developmental Psychology* 25 1 (1989): 96–108; and J. Brandstädter, and G. Renner, "Tenacious Goal Pursuit and Flexible Goal Adjustment: Explication and Age-Related Analysis of Assimilative and Accommodative Strategies of Coping," *Psychology and Aging* 5 1 (1990): 58–67.

173 Paul B. Baltes, Jacqui Smith, and Ursula Staudinger, "Wisdom and Successful Aging," in T. B. Sonderegger, ed. *Nebraska Symposium on Motivation* (Lincoln: University of Nebraska Press, in press).

173 Elliott Jaques, "Death and the Mid-Life Crisis," *International Journal of Psychoanalysis* 46 (1965): 502–14, reprinted in Elliott Jaques, *Work, Creativity and Social Justice* (New York: International Universities Press, 1970).

173 Daniel J. Levinson, et al., *The Seasons of a Man's Life* (New York: Ballantine Books, 1979).

174 Whitbourne quoted in P. Harris, and D. Lyon, "You're Not Having a Mid-Life Crisis. You Just Think You Are," *Boston Globe Magazine,* 26 November 1989. See also Susan K. Whitbourne, *The Me I Know: A Study of Adult Identity* (New York: Springer-Verlag, 1986); and Susan K. Whitbourne, et al., "Psychological Development in Adulthood; a 22-Year

Longitudinal Study," *Journal of Personality and Social Psychology,* in press.

175   Song lyrics from Al Hoffman and Maurice Sigler, "Little Man, You've Had a Busy Day" (Burbank, Calif.: Polygram International Music, copyright 1934, 1961).

Index